D1127550

The Hands of Peace

The Hands of Peace

Marione Ingram

Foreword by
Thelton Henderson

Skyhorse Publishing

Skyhorse Publishing books may be purchased in bulk at special discounts for sales promotion, corporate gifts, fund-raising, or educational purposes. Special editions can also be created to specifications. For details, contact the Special Sales Department, Skyhorse Publishing, 307 West 36th Street, 11th Floor, New York, NY 10018 or info@skyhorsepublishing.com.

Visit our website at www.skyhorsepublishing.com.

10 9 8 7 6 5 4 3 2 1

Library of Congress Cataloging-in-Publication Data is available on file.

Cover design by Brian Peterson
Cover photo courtesy of Marione Ingram

Print ISBN: 978-1-63220-289-5
Ebook ISBN: 978-1-63220-851-4

Printed in China

For the women of Mississippi who fought and are still fighting for their rights, and to Daniel.

Contents

Foreword

Imagine knowing, from the age of five, that there were people who wanted you dead. Or having to deal with frequent bombings of your hometown, but being denied entrance to a bomb shelter because you were "different." Or, while still a child, finding the strength, and the hope, to save your mother from killing herself, after she had lost all strength and given up all hope.

Those of you who have read *The Hands of War* know that I am talking about Marione Ingram, a remarkable woman who described in that book her experiences growing up Jewish in Hamburg, Germany, and how—miraculously—her immediate family survived the Holocaust. In this, her second memoir, Marione takes us on a far different journey, one that details her life of activism, which was no doubt inspired by the horrific attitudes and events that robbed her of any sense of childhood, experiences that taught her what it was like to be the target of discrimination.

I first met Marione over fifty years ago outside a Chinese take-out place in Washington, DC, where I was working as an attorney with the United States Department of Justice. She and her husband, Daniel, happened to know the person I was waiting to dine with, and we made quick introductions and struck up an easy conversation. Daniel and Marione were quite interested in the work I was doing at the time, which involved voting rights in the very much still-segregated South, and I was curious to learn more about their backgrounds and what led to their deep interest in social justice.

Soon, I found myself invited to their home, which was a magnet for civil rights activists like James Baldwin, Harry Belafonte, Marion Barry, and others, not only for the discourse that occurred there, but also because it was a joyful place. Marione would later tell me that this was one of the major differences between the Holocaust and the civil rights movement: Jews during the Holocaust had no cause for celebration, but those fighting for civil rights often found joy in their work while, at the same time, participating in acts of defiance that were at times quite dangerous and always courageous. In *The Hands of Peace*, Marione shares many of the rich stories from that time period, and we also learn about how she and Daniel became so frustrated with the Reagan administration that they sold their home in the United States and moved abroad in protest.

A child who never gave up hope, Marione became an activist who shared her inherent optimism with everyone with whom she came into contact. Her inspiration and determination were infectious, and the stories she shares in the pages that follow will, I hope, continue to spread her message: a message about not giving up on what is right, about fighting for what you believe in, and about living a life full of intention and without regret.

Thank you, Marione, for sharing yourself with the world.

—Thelton Henderson

Preface

Unlike the Holocaust, which claimed the lives of millions of Europeans in the 1940s, the American civil rights movement twenty years later changed the lives of millions for the better. It was my misfortune to be among the European victims of racism, and my great good fortune to later play a small but impassioned role in a nonviolent movement to empower American victims of racism. I was grateful for the opportunity to join hands with others in a movement for social justice that eventually transformed me more completely than it transformed America. I stopped being a surviving victim of genocide and war and became an activist opponent of both.

Growing up, I couldn't possibly know that I was simultaneously experiencing Germany's attempt to exterminate all European Jews and the deadliest man-made firestorm in history. But the people responsible for both knew, and they knew it was wrong. Everyone knows that no cause has the right to kill children for any reason whatsoever, and that collective enforcement of such a law would severely limit most of the evil that men do. Yet racism, fanaticism, and greed trump child protection even in the primary-school classrooms of a military superpower.

In the civil rights movement, there were hundreds of known and unknown heroes, people who were beaten nearly to death and didn't quit, who were imprisoned and jailed dozens of times, not knowing whether they would get out alive; people whose homes and churches were bombed , who lost jobs and loved ones; people who were shadowed by known assassins, lived every day for years under threat, who could not rely on the police or courts for anything but abuse and were expected to remain pacific, patient, and sane in the face of society's schizophrenic apprehension of equality.

I was not one of those heroes. At times I shared space in the same leaky boat, but with skin tones that would have given me privileged access to a limited number of life preservers. I had, however, come directly from a hell that was even more deranged, cruel, and lethal, and much better organized for genocide. It is because of that perspective and the insight it provides into racism's ability to create ever more terrible conditions that I invite readers to continue.

—Marione Ingram

Chapter One

Love and War

I didn't want to go back, and I couldn't tell Daniel why. I couldn't tell myself why. Perhaps the story of Orpheus and Eurydice had made too much of an impression on me as a child. Orpheus looked back at Eurydice while leading her out of Hades, and she was forced to return to the land of the dead forever because Satan had told Orpheus: Don't look back! But I knew that Eurydice's tragic fate wasn't the reason I was unresponsive whenever Daniel, my husband and lover for more than fifty years, wondered aloud what life was like today in Mississippi. When I had gone there in 1964, I'd felt like I was entering America's Heart of Darkness. Having escaped alive, I was still afraid almost fifty years later of what I would see if I went back.

Perhaps I felt about Mississippi the way I felt about Germany years after its defeat and my flight to America. Without pressuring me, Daniel had somehow persuaded me to go back to Germany when, for me, it was still Nazi Germany even though forty years had passed since the official end of World War II. We went to Hamburg in 1985 on an overnight ferry from England, intending to stay only long enough to purchase a car. The plan was for us to drive from there to Tuscany where we would live while Daniel wrote the great

American civil rights novel. I would make art while he was doing this, surrounded by timeless beauty and immersed in a culture as stimulating and warm as the region's red wine and brilliant sunshine.

We had sold our home in Washington, DC, to make the move, but on our first night in Europe I discovered a lump in my breast. So as soon as I reached Hamburg, I contacted a former classmate, who arranged for me to see a specialist she trusted. Daniel and I were riding on a Hamburg tram to see the doctor when I suddenly began vomiting uncontrollably. Daniel managed to get me to the doctor's office where I explained that I hadn't lost my lunch because I was afraid I had cancer, but because my gut fear of German doctors had literally erupted after lying dormant for many years.

That fear had been implanted early when my mother told me that Nazi law forbade doctors to help premature Jewish babies survive, and I had arrived earlier than expected and needed help. Fortunately, a doctor at Hamburg's Jewish Hospital had refused to obey Nazi rules. Soon after the war, however, I learned that thousands of Jewish children had been condemned to death by concentration camp doctors and that, at a medical facility near where we lived in Hamburg, doctors had performed cruel experiments on Jewish girls, whom they killed just before British troops entered the city. So it was not only a great relief to learn that the lump in my breast was benign, it was eye-opening to discover that lab results were provided immediately and that the doctor was more careful and considerate than any of the doctors who had treated me for cysts in America.

My experience with the German doctor suggested that even history's sickest nation might heal over time; but it didn't neutralize my deeply felt anger created by the Holocaust and postwar anti-Semitism. That anger, suppressed but still volatile, survived several happy and productive decades I had in America and Italy. It also survived seven years in Hamburg, where I discovered that I could be productive and happy as long as Daniel was there with me.

I had returned to Hamburg from Italy near the end of the bloody twentieth century to complete a book about my family's experience during the Nazi era. I wanted the book to be a memorial to those who were killed and a tribute to unsung heroes like my father and his brothers, who were not Jews but suffered beatings, imprisonment, torture, and, for some, death trying to help us and others. I also wanted readers to know what it was like to be a child inside an exploding firestorm, surrounded by the charred bodies of thousands of children killed by Allied bombers. And I fervently hoped that sharing such experiences would encourage more people to challenge calls for war and acts of war, especially those that take the lives of children.

It was a book I had begun many years earlier in an attempt to tame some of the internal demons that bedeviled my sleep and caused me to cringe and quaver when sirens began to wail or even when there was talk on the radio about the possibility of war. I wasn't generally fearful or unhappy. On the contrary, I felt safer than ever and truly relished the freedom and excitement of being young and on my own in New York. But my dreams were haunted by images of buildings and people on fire, and a sudden loud noise or the sight or sound of a fire engine might make me panic and want to hide. I thought that writing about the experiences that still disturbed me might help me get over them. Every afternoon in the late fifties, Hilda, the owner of Caffe Reggio on MacDougal Street, which was around the corner from where Daniel and I lived on Minetta Lane, would reserve her best table for me. It was in the far corner of the restaurant, by the window, surrounded by paintings in the style of the Italian Renaissance, and across the room from the largest, shiniest, and most splendidly ornamental espresso machine in Manhattan. In these congenial surroundings, it was virtually impossible to recall what I needed to write about, the event that British military historian Keith Lowe says "we now know to be the worst single bombing raid of the European war, and the greatest man-made firestorm the world has ever seen." But my demons were too clever to expose themselves to the light. Day after day I sat and stared at a lined yellow notepad, baffled by my inability to put on paper what was locked in memory.

This writing block remained solid until one night in Daniel's arms. Weeping and shaking, I told him the unimaginable details of ten days and nights of punitive air strikes against Hamburg, code-named Operation Gomorrah. Talking until dawn, I also recalled my mother's attempted suicide three days before the bombing started, and the way I felt when I found her unconscious with her head in our unlit oven. She was fully recovered and awake on the warm summer night when Operation Gomorrah began, heralded by an incredibly beautiful display of flares that hung in the sky like huge stars and then slowly descended as beams from powerful searchlights that probed the clouds for bombers. That image, which remains fresh and available to me, was followed by the terrifying screams of bombs with high-decibel whistles attached to their fins, each scream ending with a deafening explosion, and some powerful enough to destroy a block of apartment buildings or an entire hospital.

But as those who planned Operation Gomorrah had calculated, the most effective way to kill more than fifty thousand civilians in three or so hours was to shower the ancient city's residential districts with enough incendiary bombs to create an all-consuming firestorm. I remembered the direct hit on our apartment building and being denied entry to a bomb shelter by our neighbors because we were Jews, and to a church for the same reason. I also remembered the countless horrors that followed and some unexpected kindnesses, even what dress and panties I wore throughout the ordeal.

At Caffe Reggio in the days following that night in Daniel's arms, I set down on paper what I had remembered, which seemed to somewhat pacify the demons, and helped me to keep or regain my composure even when there was news about war or events that might lead to war. Daniel, who wrote about labor relations laws for a large publishing house, was encouraging of my effort to dampen enthusiasm for warfare by writing about aspects of WWII that few Americans seemed to know. But writing about war and genocide was not nearly as healing and helpful as being in love, starting a family, and combating racism nonviolently in the American civil rights movement. Caught up in such exciting endeavors in the early sixties, I put the book aside and let it gather dust as the civil rights movement melded with the antiwar and antipoverty movements and helped to inspire the women's rights movement. Participation in these movements was fulfilling as well as demanding, and I returned to making art—mainly constructions, paintings, and fiber creations—refreshed and inspired by experience and by the expanded appreciation of contemporary art that had accompanied social change.

I took up the manuscript again in the nineties, not only because I wanted to honor my parents and others who were no longer alive, but also because it was apparent that so-called civilized nations had learned little from a century of wars and genocide. I wanted to add my voice to those who say "never again" and mean never kill anyone, including enemies, unless it's absolutely necessary to do so to prevent them from killing. After an excerpt from my work-in-progress was published in Great Britain and the United States by *Granta* magazine, I felt ecstatic reading the conclusion of a positive review of it by *The Guardian*. It read, "Perhaps if those who fund and profit from wars cared to read memories such as these, the expectations of this new century might be just a little brighter."

I called the completed book about my family's experience of war and genocide *The Hands of War.* Like the *Granta* excerpt, which was also published in Russia and in the 2007 edition of *The Best American Essays,* the book received positive reviews. After its publication in the spring of 2013, I believed that all my demons had been laid to rest. But that was when Daniel began to wonder aloud about conditions in Mississippi, more specifically about life in

Moss Point and Pascagoula, the tiny cities on the Gulf Coast where I had lived and worked in 1964. My reluctance to find out how things were there wasn't because I didn't care or thought it would be dangerous to find out or assumed that everything there was just fine. I cared, and I didn't think white Mississippians were nearly as hostile to meddling activists as they had been in the sixties. My reluctance was rooted in a fear that I'd find out that the rights we won in the sixties had never been allowed to take effect.

Living in Europe in the eighties and nineties, we had been heartened by reports of African Americans being elected to high offices even in southern states, but we had lost touch with our friends in Mississippi and had almost no news of what was happening there. Soon after returning to DC in 2007, we campaigned for Barack Obama in nearby Virginia and were delirious when he won the election, carrying both Virginia and North Carolina, two southern states in which race is normally a major factor. It seemed that the moral arc of history had indeed bent toward justice. In short order, however, it became clear that the election of an African American president had not signaled the death of political racism, but its reconstruction in the guise of anti-government animus. The ideological coating of fiscal conservatism was as transparent as the paint covering the N-word on the huge rock at the entrance to Governor Rick Perry's Texas ranch.

Even before Daniel suggested that we go south in 2013, I had become alarmed by the new voter identification measures and other restrictions being pushed through state legislatures to discourage voting by African American and Hispanics. One didn't have to have grown up in Germany to know that by blocking rivals from voting on key issues, the Nazis had turned a democratic government into a one-party state. I didn't say this aloud because it was clear that any comparison with that history would be considered over the top, and it wouldn't have helped for me to point out that the Nazi agenda had been dismissed as ridiculously far-fetched up until the time it became a fait accompli.

Despite the enactment of new voting eligibility or identification requirements in such bastions of liberty as Philadelphia, I tried to take comfort from the so-called checks and balances and the existence of an "independent judiciary." But when five unabashed activists in black robes decided that corporations were just folks and entitled to buy elections in order to exercise their Constitutional right to free speech, I suspected that we had entered a new era of corporate fascism. And when the gang of five shortly after gutted the Voting Rights Act by declaring that it was no longer needed despite the fact that Congress had recently reauthorized it, I agreed with Daniel; it was time to take a look at how the Mississippians I had loved and whose struggle I had embraced were faring almost fifty years later. Alas, Mr. William and Mrs. Lottie Scott, with whom I'd lived, and other elders who had challenged white rule would no longer be there. But some of the children who had attended the Freedom School might remember the civil rights struggle and tell me how, if at all, it had affected their lives.

Chapter Two

In the Beginning

Although I didn't realize it at the time, my first journey to Mississippi began in Hamburg, where my father had instilled in me the idea that because I survived the Nazi era, it was my sacred and secular duty to oppose racism wherever I encountered it. I knew he was right—an atheist gentile, he had been beaten and imprisoned, had lost his business and nearly his life, all for helping Jews—but I disliked being so indoctrinated at the time. I was having great difficulty as the only Jew in a school with teachers who were ex-Nazis and students who blamed me for the fact that they couldn't be Hitler Youth. In fact, I was still deeply angry at him for making me stand up to them until, not two weeks before my seventeenth birthday, I said goodbye and boarded an Italian liner sailing to New York. My mother was living there with her new husband and my youngest sister.

Little more than a year later, my mother had moved to Los Angeles and I was completely on my own, feasting on New York's matchless creativity and profoundly grateful that no one seemed to care whether I or anyone else was a Jew. Since I had been classified by my so-called homeland as a subhuman and would have been exterminated if my fellow countrymen had had their way, I didn't much care for my national identity. I considered myself to be stateless and obtained a passport as a "citizen of the world" from an organization in Chicago that promised to contribute the purchase price to poor children. I also enrolled in a United Nations class in Esperanto, a proposed "universal language," and was disappointed for more than one reason when the class was cancelled, because fewer than a dozen people signed up. Having studied British English in Hamburg and Switzerland, I had an accent that was recognizably foreign but not easily identified by non-Europeans. Often asked where I came from, I usually avoided giving a straight answer, letting people guess and not correcting them when they were wrong or confirming their answer when they were correct. If pressed, I might encourage a new acquaintance to think I had been born in France and later forced to live in Germany—anything to keep from being lumped with the people who had tried to kill me and my family. In any case, it didn't seem to matter where I came from. The people who asked were merely curious.

It soon became clear, however, that Americans cared a lot about where people of color lived and worked. I suppose most foreigners who were not forewarned were surprised to find out how ghettoized New York and many other US cities were. But it wasn't something New Yorkers talked about, at least to me. They seemed to think it was natural that all "Negroes" would live in Harlem. I learned how difficult it was for blacks to live anywhere else at about the same time I learned how difficult it was for them to get jobs outside Harlem that were not menial. Without any particular qualifications, I had landed an internship at a large advertising firm with clients in the world of fashion, as well as the worlds of cars, toothpaste, and soap flakes. In addition to learning some of the secrets of commercial art and buyer motivation, I developed a friendship with an attractive young woman a few years older and far better educated than I was. She was black, she had a university degree, and she was the ladies' room attendant at my firm. Joan explained that her job was the best a woman of color could hold there.

When I protested this obvious discrimination to my boss and his boss, I was told that, in the absence of special circumstances, the firm's employment policy adhered to trade practice on Madison Avenue. I pointed out that only a short time ago, everybody had been outraged by the case of Emmett Till, a black teenager who was murdered in Mississippi for supposedly winking at a white woman, and whose killers had been allowed to walk free. Terribly upset by the crime, I had talked with almost everyone I knew about it and had been assured that this sort of thing could only happen in the Deep South. New Yorkers weren't like that, they said. Suggesting any connection between the firm's employment policy and southern racism often elicited indignation. But after I resigned in protest, a few men told me privately that they also thought the policy was wrong.

Joan appreciated my protest and the precariousness of my financial situation after I quit. She invited me to her place in Harlem on weekends and introduced me to some of the fabulous nightlife activities and people she knew, all of whom seemed to have ironic stories to share about white people's racial hypocrisy and hypocritical black responses to it—all of which struck us as hilarious. On occasion I heard a jazz great, or an unknown with great talent, jam with a small combo in an after-hours dive. At first Joan didn't find it funny that I was inexperienced but eager to have an affair if I found the right man. That man had been described for me by my mother, who had ruled out young men and had insisted that the person suitable for me have maturity, sensitivity, and idealism. That made him virtually impossible for me to find. Joan smiled at this, but didn't mess with Mother's caveats. She cracked up, however, when I told her about being taken by a date to a small Swiss chalet in New Jersey.

The man, who despite Mother's wishes was young, had a car of his own and had driven me to various places, including a polo match in Connecticut and a beach on Long Island, and had never pressed his desire to have sex. So when he suggested one evening that we go to a "motel," I readily agreed although I didn't know what that word meant. I remained cheerfully expectant as we drove through desolate New Jersey marshes and then along a maze of side roads toward something I couldn't quite envision. When we came to a halt in front of a simulated Swiss skiing chalet with a steeply pitched roof and a pink neon sign that read "MEADOWLARK MOTEL," I became very confused. There were several smaller ersatz chalets leading away from the larger one into which my date disappeared for several minutes, emerging with a boyish grin and a key attached to a triangular piece of plastic. We then parked in front of one of the small chalets and he ushered me into a room with a very large bed and very little else. He sat on the bed, bounced himself a couple of times, patted the garish green and white chenille coverlet, and pointed to a wooden door beside a knotty pine wardrobe.

"Would you like to use the bathroom?" he asked, looking a little nervous but happier than I had ever seen him.

In a state of total panic I took refuge in the bathroom and opened its tiny window to reduce the nauseating smell of pine oil. To regain composure, I splashed my face with cold water, not caring that my mascara might run. Looking into the dingy mirror, I rehearsed what I would say when I went back into the bedroom and faced my companion. But I almost forgot my lines when I saw that he had already undressed down to his bulging undershorts.

"I'm sorry," I said, trying to remain calm, "but I honestly didn't know what a motel was when you asked me. I wouldn't have come if I had known. I can't possibly do what you want here. If you try to force me, you might succeed but you won't like it and I'll hate it. I'll repay you for what this has cost you, but please, please let's go back to New York."

He looked almost as stunned as I had been. But angry! So angry that I thought he might attack me, or explode. But after a few expletives, he didn't say another word. All the way back across the

New Jersey meadows he was so coldly furious that I thought he was going to stop the car and put me out. When we reached Manhattan, I offered to get out at the nearest subway stop, but he drove me all the way to my building. When I tried to apologize again, he silently reached across me and opened the door. I got out and never saw or heard from him again, and after that I never accepted an invitation to go somewhere until I knew what sort of place I was going to and what I was expected to do there.

Realizing that neither my mother nor the mean German girls I had gone to school with had imparted much in the way of practical advice about sex, Joan tactfully tried to fill in some of the blanks. She insisted that I go to a Margaret Sanger Clinic, there being one in Harlem and one not far from where I lived in lower Manhattan. She suggested that it would be better if I pretended to be married when I went there, and offered to lend me the wedding band she wore on special occasions to make men think she had a protector.

The next time I saw Joan I told her I had decided to take her advice and go to the Margaret Sanger Clinic because a doctor I had seen about my painful periods said I had bone spurs and would likely die trying to give birth if I got pregnant. I felt flush when I told Joan this, having just earned a hundred dollars for being in a fashion photo shoot, and was even wearing one of the dresses I'd modeled. So I suggested we have a champagne cocktail, my treat, at one of the fabulous hotels across the street from Central Park to continue our conversation. Joan started to protest, but we were near such a hotel and I was excited and wanted to celebrate my financial good fortune and stunning frock. However, at the first cocktail lounge we tried, the maître d' told us they didn't serve unescorted women. When we pointed out there were two unescorted women sitting nearby, we were told they were hotel guests. At the next lounge, the bartender brought me a glass of champagne but refused to serve Joan.

"If you want to drink together, take the A train," he said. I asked Joan what he meant.

"He means we should go to Harlem," Joan said. I picked up the glass, gave it to Joan, and put my hundred dollar bill on the bar as she drank it down.

"Give me another," I demanded.

"You're too young," he said, pushing back the bill. "Now get out of here before we both get in trouble." He looked like he was ready to put us out, so we left.

As we were walking out of the hotel, Joan said the bartender reminded her of a boyfriend she once had who'd lied to her with a straight face and tried to slap her when she refused to believe him. "Once, when he balled up his fist," she said, "I chased him out of my apartment with my pistol." Before entering the subway to take the A train, she took some change from her purse and gave me enough to take a train to Fourth Street in the Village, which was not far from my apartment. She also fished out the wedding band she had offered earlier. "What you really need," she said ruefully, "is my pistol."

The next morning, I phoned the Margaret Sanger Clinic for an appointment later in the day. A serious-looking woman at the clinic, who may have been Margaret Sanger, welcomed me pleasantly, glanced at my ring, and handed me a lengthy form to fill out. I soon realized that I was almost as unprepared as I had been at the New Jersey motel. In addition to asking how long I had been married, the clinic wanted to know how often my husband and I had intercourse and how many times per day. I had no hesitancy in answering that we had been married one year, and reported that we had intercourse every day. But I had no idea how many times one did it. Figuring that I would want to make love for at least an hour and more likely two, and that it might take five to ten minutes to climax, I wrote that we had intercourse twelve to fifteen times per day.

I began to wonder whether I had answered correctly when a woman in a doctor's coat asked me the same how-many-times questions while she gave me a vaginal examination that caused me to wince and her to look almost as uncomfortable as I felt. She seemed to have considerable difficulty fitting me with a diaphragm but finally managed to insert one that was heavily lubricated and then to remove it without causing me too much discomfort. She then asked me to demonstrate to a nurse who was present that I could do it, too. With growing embarrassment at my ineptitude, I managed to insert and remove it two or three times. After I was on my feet and dressed, the doctor advised me to insert the diaphragm before having intercourse and to remove and clean it the next day, but to have my husband continue to use condoms as well until I returned in two weeks for a checkup. The receptionist, the doctor, and the nurse each shook my hand cordially and wished me luck as I left the clinic. I was still slightly uncomfortable and embarrassed, but pleased to be the possessor of a dome-shaped diaphragm that would protect me if I made love.

When I returned Joan's ring two weeks later, she was delighted that I had stayed the course, though she gently let me know that after the honeymoon, few married men were as active as my mythical husband. Aware that the loss of my job was forcing me to give up my pad, she said I could move in with her but that she was going to have to leave her apartment and, if possible, Harlem, because a bad-tempered former lover would soon be back on the street and demand to be taken in. So we decided to get an apartment together in a different neighborhood, preferably one that was in a building with a doorman. We checked all the advertisements and made several appointments, but everywhere we went we were told that the vacancy was no longer available, despite the fact that the same rental agents had told me on the phone only minutes earlier that the places were unrented. No agent would admit it, but when I asked a doorman if his building was for whites only, he gave me a look that said, "What? Are you dumb or something?" Then he nodded his head and touched two fingers to the visor of his cap to indicate that the interview was over. Still, we continued to look, expanding our reach and lowering our requirements until, finally, we were told that we could have an apartment but only if it was in my name alone and Joan was listed as my servant or caregiver. When we heard this, we'd had enough. We refused the place and gave up looking. It seemed futile to continue searching for a place where we'd be comfortable. I'd also landed a job in the film division of the Museum of Modern Art. It didn't pay much, but I could walk to work and keep my pad. Even better, I got to know some of the great curators at the museum and several of the artists and exhibiters in orbit, including talented unknowns, some of whom I shared a studio with. Plus, my work included shepherding distinguished patrons or visitors given private access to the film collection. Through this I met wonderful people such as Eleanor Roosevelt, Greta Garbo, and Jean Renoir. For more than a year, I believed MOMA was the ideal place for me to work—then Nelson Rockefeller's tight-fistedness finally got to me and I returned his ten-dollar Christmas bonus in an impertinent personal protest of inadequate pay.

During the years I worked at the museum, I met the kind of man my mother had prescribed for me. Daniel and I met at a party in the Village apartment building where he was living at the time. I had been invited, but Daniel, who didn't know the host, had crashed the party after seeing me walk down a flight of stairs on the arm of my date to attend it. It wasn't at all like him to do this, but he felt he needed to meet me. I was well dressed but pencil slim, lacking the curves that might entice a mild-mannered man to abandon common courtesy and invade another man's turf, to come between a couple. But that's what happened. Daniel contrived an obviously transparent ruse to get into the party, and, once in, accepted the host's offer of a drink, walked across the room to where Michael and I were sitting, and joined us. After talking with him for more than an hour, it occurred to me that if I should ever decide to marry, it would be to someone like him, someone witty who cared about people and the arts and made me feel he was interested in everything about me. I didn't try to analyze it then, but when he left the party for a few minutes, I felt that I couldn't bear it if we never saw one another again. When he returned, he had a rare lithograph with him and gave it to me. It was his most precious work of art. He also gave me a copy of George Orwell's *Homage to Catalonia*. As if I was an observer or reading a scene in a play, I heard myself invite him to come to my apartment after midnight, by which time my companion would have taken me home and departed.

When I arrived for work at MOMA the next morning, I went first to my friend Angela, a discerning woman of the world, or so I thought, and asked her if she noticed anything different about me. She asked if I was wearing a new dress and I told her it was something more important that I would explain later. But when I entered my office in the museum's film department, my boss, a cultivated gay bachelor in his sixties, didn't have to be asked. He took one look and said that he knew what I had done last night. When I pressed him to tell me how he knew, he would only say, "I can see it in your eyes."

In the following weeks and months, every part of me celebrated uncovering more of Daniel as he uncovered more of me, and discovering that making love was not only more glorious than I had imagined, it got even better over time. In various ways, sometimes unintentionally, we revealed our core convictions, inner fears, defenses, and aspirations. Although we had traveled very different paths, we had arrived at many similar conclusions and loved and loathed most of the same things. We enjoyed our differences though, and didn't wish to change one another. We thought it uncanny how well our views and tastes, and bodies, intertwined.

Daniel had grown up in Tennessee on the campus of a private military academy with the ridiculously romantic name of Castle Heights. His father was the commandant there, the incarnation of discipline for faculty and cadets. Daniel and his father loved and respected one another, but Daniel was a maverick who didn't sound or think like the other white southerners he grew up with. His long experience with militarism, both in the school and in the army in Japan, where he tried as a lawyer to keep soldiers out of prison, had made him deeply distrustful of authoritarian institutions. He also loved and respected his mother, a novelist whose stories about family dissonance in rural Tennessee at the turn of the century were in the *New Yorker* and other magazines. But Daniel and his parents had strong, sometimes irreconcilable, differences about race, authority, and the social order. By local standards, however, they were moderates, and Daniel's father and a colleague once broke up a lynch mob by brandishing their military sabers.

Daniel didn't tell me he loved me until one morning when he showed up at my apartment shortly after dawn, having spent the night in the company of his closest friends. He confessed that he had been in love with me for some time but had wanted to be absolutely certain about it before saying so and asking me to move in with him. The preceding hours had been a sort of farewell to single life, he explained. But while he wanted to move in together, he was not proposing something as irrelevant and unnecessary as marriage. Mutual will rather than legal or holy writ would cement our relationship. I told him I loved him and wholeheartedly concurred that marriage was superfluous. That day I moved into his place on Minetta Lane, an angled street boxed by Sixth Avenue and MacDougal Street, West Third Street and Bleecker Street.

At the time I was not on very good terms with my father, mainly because he had been so overprotective after Mother went to America, leaving me with him in Hamburg. He wouldn't let me date any boy unless he approved of him and what we would be doing together. In addition, there had to be an adult around to serve as a chaperon. On the Italian liner to America, I learned at the end of the voyage that he had even bribed my steward and the chief steward to make sure I didn't do anything improper. I really resented his restrictions, which I interpreted as misplaced mistrust, even more than I'd resented being sent to a school full of anti-Semites. So now, being twenty-one, self-sufficient, and in love, I wrote a letter cataloging and criticizing what I considered to be examples of his overly restrictive parenting, and informing him that I was now happier than I had ever been because I was living with a man whom I adored and who adored me. Of course I also told him things about Daniel that I knew he would like, such as that he was caring and helpful to others as well as to me.

To my surprise, my father wrote back a seven-page letter saying he was glad that I was happily in love and living with a man deserving of respect. He explained that he had long believed that it was foolish for people to get married who had only known one another when they were at their best. He said couples should "first live skin on skin," so that she knows what he is like when he is tired, unshaven, hungry, and loses his temper; and he knows what she is like when angry, unkempt, disappointed, or experiencing her monthly cycle. He admitted to being a maladroit single father, gently mentioning by way of mitigation that I was always extremely willful and impossible to predict. In response to my lament that Mother had left me with him in Europe when she went to America, he reminded me that I mustn't ever even think unkindly about that, because of what had been done to her family. He added that he had recognized when I was still an infant that I had an independent nature that would never be guided by what others, including parents, said I should do. This was the beginning of a new and beautiful relationship between us, conducted mainly by post, that would age like the brandy he so enjoyed; and I would continue to be enriched after his death by learning about truly heroic things he had done and endured to help Jews.

I also wrote my mother, not to complain but to let her know that I was in love with and living with a man who met all of her exacting criteria—sensitive, mature, caring, attentive, intelligent, etc. I assured her that I was not only happy but also secure in the strength of my relationship. Her reply was not censorious, but she rather breezily asked what had become of an earlier boyfriend. In time she would appreciate how fortunate it was that Daniel and I found one another.

Every time they burned something in the kitchen of the Minetta Tavern, we caught some of the smoke through the window of our apartment. But we had our own fireplace and an endless supply of free flowers from a florist shop that fronted for a bookie joint. The bookie had an overabundance of unsold flowers that might arouse suspicions, and I was exceedingly happy to help him out. Also, our building was integrated. African Americans who worked in the Village might find a place to live there if they found out about a vacancy before it was listed and offered some under-the-table money, as Daniel had. For a rent-controlled apartment—our rent was $50 per month—inside a gated courtyard in that desirable location, a small bribe was totally acceptable. On our first New Year's Eve together, Daniel and I had a lobster dinner at a Village restaurant followed by a performance of *The Threepenny Opera*, with Lotte Lenya as Jenny Diver. (Ever after Minetta Lane was "Dock Street"—where Jenny lived with "Mack the Knife"—and our apartment was "that foul two-by-four where we made love.") Across the street from us was Johnny Romero's, a nightclub with two bars, a dance floor, and a garden that was open when the weather allowed. Until the Mafia destroyed it, Romero's was one of the few places, and possibly the only place south of Harlem, where blacks and whites mingled romantically in public. Directly above us lived one of Romero's bartenders, Jim, a young black social worker from South Carolina who had given up the worthy but impecunious work for which he had been trained and taken up bartending. This had allowed him to satisfy his sexual fantasies with a seemingly endless supply of affluent women in their forties.

One evening I knocked at Jim's apartment door in a panic and was startled to see that he was entertaining three such women in various stages of undress. I was there because Daniel was not home and I had been pursued down MacDougal Street by a stalker who grabbed my wrist as I entered the courtyard in front of our three-story building. "Nobody likes me," he said as I twisted out of his grip and ran into our building and up the stairs. Jim, who was not particularly good-looking but was obviously catnip to these women, left me with them while he chased away the stalker. The next day we learned that the stalker had later accosted and killed a New York University librarian who was walking to the subway stop a block from us at Sixth Avenue and Fourth Street. An obvious psychopath, he had stabbed the librarian when she wouldn't have anything to do with him.

When Jim's lovely mother would visit from South Carolina, his powder-blue Cadillac convertible would be parked out of sight and Daniel and I would be invited to dinner at his apartment, during which the demands of his career as a social worker dominated the genteel table talk. Lucky Jim also had a vivacious African American lover, a young woman who wanted him to change his ways and marry her. We met the woman, Ginger, when she stopped on our landing one night while pursuing Jim, who thundered ahead of her down all three flights and into the courtyard with his pants unclosed and shirt half on. We opened our door and saw her bent over trying to catch a last glimpse of Jim as he finished dressing, regained composure, and then nonchalantly walked to work. Meanwhile, Ginger had one hand over her mouth to muffle her laughter, while the other one held a long butcher knife. Seeing us, she profusely apologized for disturbing us, smiling impishly as she explained that the knife was just a prop to let Jim know how sincerely she wanted him to stop fooling around with other women. To show solidarity, I invited her in for a glass of Portuguese rosé. After that encounter, she stopped by almost every time she visited Jim.

Ginger was a night nurse who lived and worked in Harlem, which meant that she and Jim worked roughly the same hours, except that she had every other weekend off. Like Jim, she had come to

New York from South Carolina. She wanted to get away from her very religious family and the hyperventilated church they attended and insisted she attend several times a week. In the city she hadn't altogether given up religion, but, instead, had been attracted to the Catholic Church because of the quiet dignity and beauty she found there. Although she was a born imp—Daniel saw her as a reincarnated wood nymph—Ginger loved the gilded interiors of the church, its restrained music, and its solemn rituals so much that she underwent a lengthy instruction and became a Catholic. However, she quickly ran into trouble. She didn't mind confessing from time to time that she had sinned by having sex without being married, but she objected to being continually asked how many times. She found it useless to argue with her confessor or other priests and eventually stopped confessing and attending services. She still went to a Catholic church to enjoy the surroundings, and probably pray, but she didn't change her ways. She also didn't manage to reform Jim, who was killed a few years later in what a mutual friend reported as a lovers' triangle.

I'm not sure whether, before he died, Jim was able to see the Pulitzer Prize-winning play, *No Place to Be Somebody*, written by a fellow Romero's bartender, a man who was part African American and part Native American. The play was about an African American proprietor of a New York nightclub who was crushed by a powerful Mafia don who blamed him for the drug addiction and pregnancy of the don's daughter. Daniel and I thought it was a fictionalized but fairly accurate depiction of what had happened to Romero's, which had been totally demolished after hours one night by unknown men wielding sledgehammers. For weeks following the nightclub's mysterious destruction, the Village literally buzzed with speculation about what might have caused such wrath, and I was interrogated more than once by Mafiosi posing as FBI agents or FBI agents doing the Mafia's work. They wanted to know the whereabouts of Johnny Romero, who had fled first to Cuba and later to Paris, where he opened another nightclub. Jim didn't tell us exactly what had happened, but the play later appeared to confirm what we had surmised.

In our relationship, Daniel and I enjoyed a platter-full of fictional melodrama that resembled the goings-on at Romero's. He had an after-work job as a spear-carrier at the Metropolitan Opera (the "Old Met") and, as he still likes to remind me, got to "sing" with Maria Callas and "dance" with Margot Fonteyn when the Royal Ballet came to town. For most performances, I got a standing room ticket for exactly the same amount that he was paid as a spear-carrier. We also helped a neighbor across our courtyard publicize performances by John Cage and the Merce Cunningham Dance Company. Surrounded by what was arguably the best avant- garde theater outside Dublin or London, and the best food this side of southern Italy, we read Dostoyevsky, Kafka, Hesse, Kawabata, Capote, and the *Village Voice* (until Norman Mailer was forced to resign after reviewing *Waiting for Godot* without having seen it). We also had lots of friends who were aspiring artists, writers, musicians, actors, or dancers, almost all of whom signed the petitions I (and, famously, violinist Isaac Stern) circulated to save Carnegie Hall from being demolished. Because the Hall's acoustics were superb, Daniel and I had enjoyed many concerts in the cheapest seats in the uppermost balcony, and I felt that it would be criminal to destroy such access to beautiful music. It was my first taste of protest, and despite the financial power of our opponents, people power eventually overcame.

Daniel and I were so happy in the sooty, stimulating, demi-paradise that was Manhattan in the late 1950s that we never thought about going anywhere else. But then Prentice Hall Publishing, where Daniel was a senior editor—earning half the salary of an elevator operator—moved from lower Fifth Avenue to New Jersey. Despite the complicated commute from the Village to a strike- proof—because it had its own post office—publishing factory in Bergen

County, the thought of leaving our foul two-by-four never surfaced. But then a publisher in Washington, DC, offered Daniel twice as much money to go there and write about conflict between labor and management. The money didn't impress him as much as the fact that the publisher in Washington was the top of the line in his field and the company was an employee-owned one, in which the non-supervisory employees were represented by the American Newspaper Guild. "In other words," he said, "it's much more professional and much less exploitive." We didn't say so but we believed in each other and we both believed in change. So off we went.

Chapter Three

Thank You, Dr. Black

After New York, the District of Columbia seemed like a spacious memorial park surrounding an enormous mausoleum in which, I soon learned, our self-evident truths were interred. Here and there a bronze or marble horseman brandished a saber, as if to warn the city's nonwhite majority to keep its distance. Although more people lived in DC than in seven of the states, residents were not allowed to vote for any public official. Three commissioners appointed by the president exercised powers elsewhere given to an elected mayor. Law mandated that one member of the troika be an army general, and prejudice rooted in hundreds of years of slavery and segregation ensured that all three would be white.

About the only way the commissioners could change anything, even temporarily, was to exercise their emergency police powers. The United States Congress served as Washington's city council, regulating everything from the length of rope used to hang a major offender to the length of a dog leash in the city's parks. Taxation without representation was (and remains) the rule. White southern politicians usually ran the committees that governed DC, and for many years at least one of those overseers was a former official of the Ku Klux Klan.

Of course I didn't learn how the city worked in one day. From the first day, however, it was apparent that race was the dominant factor affecting the lives of local residents. I had seen racial inequities in New York, but DC was different. Blacks outnumbered whites by two to one, but numbers didn't count. Discrimination in employment and housing was everywhere, with only a few blacks in or out of government holding professional jobs, and almost a hundred percent of local government contracts going to white firms. Not surprisingly, dire poverty seriously afflicted most black neighborhoods. Some hospitals had segregated wards and nurseries, while restaurants usually employed either only whites or only blacks as servers. Even the professional football team, which had an offensive name I won't repeat, was lily-white.

DC schools had been told by the Supreme Court to integrate years earlier, but remained almost completely segregated in the early sixties, despite the fact that federal judges in DC served as the school board. A civil rights lawsuit eventually revealed that schools in white enclaves received far greater funding than those in black neighborhoods. All public swimming pools were in white neighborhoods, and when black youths took a streetcar across the Maryland-District line to swim, not only the pool but the car line was closed.

Such injustices, and there were many others, nourished by the myth of more races than the human race, made me not only uncomfortable but exceedingly upset. There wasn't even an opera house or concert hall, except for the faux-Greek temple where the Daughters of the American Revolution allowed whites to perform. I wanted to go back to New York even though I knew that racial discrimination was a problem there also. Daniel, who had grown up in the South, thought that the ideals that made America great were more hypocritically betrayed in DC than anywhere else. But he really liked his job at the Bureau of National Affairs, a private publishing company where he wrote about labor relations law, and took an active part in the American Newspaper Guild, a union for print journalists.

Because of my experience as a Jew in Germany, I identified with black DC youths, and was pained and frightened by what was being done to them. They were not being rounded up and gassed, but they were forced to live in ghettos, given second-rate educations, denied many opportunities white youths took for granted, and generally treated as second-class citizens if not as subhumans. In a black neighborhood only a skip and a hop from the White House, an overcrowded class was held in a basement that flooded when it rained, and rats competed for access to lunch bags. There was no playground at the school nor in the neighborhood.

Having been mistreated by teachers and students when I was finally allowed to attend school after the war, my youthful revenge fantasies resurfaced and I imagined doing all sorts of things to racists, such as administering a magical but not entirely painless shock treatment that would rearrange their brains to make them love their neighbor. Unfortunately, that was not possible; but fortunately, other people with similarly strong feelings had begun to attack DC's institutional racism. Like us, they probably had been amazed by the earlier success of a bus boycott by black residents of Montgomery, Alabama, and were inspired by recent examples of youths, most of them black college students, and adults who were challenging various forms of racial segregation or exclusion in several southern cities and towns.

These new protests appeared to be spontaneous and isolated, but there were several common threads. For one, the protesters' demands usually were very modest. They wanted access to water fountains, lunch counters, waiting rooms, parks, beaches, movies, and such. Some wanted access to public schools and others merely asked for textbooks, band instruments, or repairs to their schools. In almost every case the protesters remained nonviolent, dignified, and respectful of public order. But the white public and authorities usually reacted with outrageous hostility and, frequently, with violence. Only the protesters were punished. Even those who disapproved of civil disobedience, as many blacks and whites did, might admire the protesters' courage in risking their necks for relatively small gains.

Daniel had left his home in the South, feeling that the tenets of white-supremacy that infused and enforced just about every aspect of life there would suffocate and eventually kill him if he stayed. I had left Germany with even stronger feelings of outrage, victimization, and impotence. So when we learned that a local chapter of the Congress of Racial Equality (CORE) was challenging discrimination in the nation's capital, we welcomed the opportunity to join in. Without benefit of immersion, sprinkling of water, or other ceremony, we were soon transformed from being disapproving spectators of racial injustice into active instigators of organized resistance. It was both liberating and exhilarating.

One of our first actions was to protest the so-called "man-in-the-house rule," which denied public assistance to needy households that included a father, husband, son, or male lover more than fifteen years old. Children were forced to go hungry and families to split up because of the widely-shared racist notion that lazy black males lived indulgently on the welfare intended to help women and children. To underscore our point, we demonstrated on Mother's Day and Father's Day. But this heartbreaking, home-wrecking rule, which sometimes caused church ministers and social workers to advise husbands to leave their indigent families, was championed for DC by West Virginia's Senator Robert Byrd, whom the *Washington Post* identified as a former KKK official. As the chairman of a committee with a stranglehold on DC's finances, he saw to it that we had more welfare investigators than seven cities of comparable size combined. Not surprisingly, many if not most investigators were his constituents, and many DC police were white constituents of a powerful congressman from Virginia. But with no political clout, the campaigns to get rid of the man-in-the house rule and have a more representative police force didn't get very far very fast.

As I became increasingly active in protests against discrimination, Daniel became increasingly fearful that I might develop visa problems and be forced to leave the land of the free. Given my temperament, he thought it likely that I would break laws that I considered unjust but the authorities considered unassailable, especially by an alien. Even if I didn't engage in civil disobedience, he reasoned, if I succeeded in sufficiently annoying them, they might decide that I was an undesirable alien because I was "living in sin." Americans are easily offended by the sexual conduct of people they disapprove of, he said, pointing out that the black descendants of George Washington and Thomas Jefferson could more than fill a Virginia church, but if any of them married a white person, they and the spouse could be sent to prison.

He continued to talk earnestly about the possibility that I would be deported and various other disadvantages of our being unmarried, such as my exclusion from his employee health insurance and other benefits, getting more and more far-fetched without coming to any conclusion. Finally, I put my fingertips on his lips to stop him. We hadn't talked about marriage for more than a year and then only to disavow any interest in it. The idea that church or state or any other third party could define or alter our relationship was absurd. But suddenly, I was excited and eager to hear him come to the point.

"Are you proposing?" I asked, trying to sound slightly incredulous.

"Yes, if that's what you want!" he said, emphasizing "you" to make it sound as if marriage was my idea, not his. After a two-second pause, we both started laughing.

A few days later we took a bus from Washington, DC, to Rockville, Maryland, and got off at a grassy hamlet a dozen miles away, where we thought we could obtain a marriage license and be married on the spot. That way Daniel would only miss a few hours of work and we would get the simplest, fastest, least expensive wedding possible.

But after we got the license, we were told that we had to get married in a church to have it performed the same day. So we walked a few blocks to the nearest church, a Victorian-looking structure with white wooden columns along a narrow side porch. We knocked on the door and waited until it was opened partway by a portly man with gray hair, blue eyes, and a direct manner. He asked what we wanted and we told him we wanted to get married, then and there.

The man looked us over and examined the license, then asked us to come in. Entering through a long corridor, we stood beside a large ornate hall tree with a mirror that reflected dimly, like a forest pond, and introduced ourselves. The man, who was dressed informally, did the same.

"I'm Dr. Black," he said.

In honey-dark tones, he asked if we were Episcopalians, directing the question first to Daniel, who replied that he was but hadn't been to church in years. Dr. Black then turned to me.

"How about you, young lady?"

I told him that I wasn't an Episcopalian, leaving unsaid the fact that I am a Jew and don't practice that religion either, considering that was none of his business and not wanting to be turned away. In a softer voice, he asked if I had any intention of becoming an Episcopalian. I told him that I didn't.

"Well, no matter," he said, "You seem like a couple who ought to get married. I'll marry you, but I can't do it today. You will have to come back tomorrow night at eight. And be sure to bring a ring . . . . One for each of you if you wish." He then said goodbye and disappeared into the church.

We went home a bit annoyed that we would have to make the trip from Washington to Rockville again—but it wasn't a big deal, we told one another, since the next day would be a Saturday. It helped that Dr. Black seemed to be simpatico; in fact, we both rather liked him. That evening, we decided to get into the spirit of the occasion and invited three close friends to join us the next day. All three were men, bachelors, longtime friends of Daniel's, who had become my friends as well. Jim lived in New York, from which we had recently moved, Jack in Baltimore, and Neal in Washington.

Saturday, March 21, at five p.m., Jack arrived with Neal and Jim and loads of champagne in Jack's car, a dented, somewhat scruffy blue sedan. Daniel and I had garnered bread, cheese, pâté, and lobster salad from the French market, and so we feasted until, suddenly, we had to race to reach the church by eight. Near the district line, Daniel shouted for Jack to stop the car, jumped out, returned with a huge bunch of anemones, and whispered to me that he only had seventeen cents left.

Arriving fifteen minutes late and slightly tipsy, we found Dr. Black also in good spirits, and pleased that we had brought friends. He asked them to make themselves comfortable in a pleasant reception room and ushered Daniel and me into a book-lined office that smelled of cigar smoke and brandy. Sitting in front of a polished, antique desk, Daniel looked self-assured and handsome, but I felt as nervous as a job applicant with no experience. Dr. Black filled an imposing high-backed chair, his fingers touching together lightly in a gesture I assumed to be priestly, and directed blue eyes enlarged by rimless glasses first at Daniel and then at me.

"When I was a bachelor," he began, taking a long cigar and lighting it, "I was very happy with my life. I was a chaplain in the Navy during the war and I listened to other men complain, but I had no complaints. I was never lonely. Even after the war I had lots of companions. I enjoyed my work and I liked things the way they were. I didn't get married until I was forty-nine years old. But once I was married, I wished I had been born married!"

Having expressed precisely how I hoped to feel for the rest of my life, Dr. Black let his smile stretch his leathery cheeks. "For you two, I wish the same happiness," he said.

After pausing to puff the cigar, he continued, "At times like this, my colleagues like to lecture young couples on sex and procreation. Most of them emphasize the spiritual aspect of sex and say it should be approached with a certain reverence. I admit they may have a point. Some go so far as to say sex should only be for procreation. And procreation is important. But I say be lusty in your sex. Be lusty! God must have meant for us to enjoy sex, or he wouldn't have made it so pleasurable. Be good to one another and be loving. But be lusty! And let procreation take care of itself!"

We couldn't repress our smiles, and Dr. Black looked very pleased with himself. Removing his glasses, he turned to me, his manner serious and confidential. "There may be times, young lady," he said, "not now, but in a few years, when your man will want to make love and you won't feel like it. Don't worry about it; it's natural to feel that way. But if you can, you ought to go along with his desires. Because there may come a time in later years when you will want to make love and he won't feel like it."

Dr. Black then turned to Daniel: "If that day comes, young man, I expect that you will do your duty. These are not things to worry about, however. Just remember that Dr. Black said for you to be lusty!"

He asked if we had any questions, but we were too amused and amazed to risk speaking. After we rejoined our friends, we were surprised to be taken into the arched nave of the large church. I had thought we would be married in some smaller, less formal part of the building, especially since I wasn't Episcopalian. We were such a small party, and the church was vast and ornate. I noticed that there were banks of fresh flowers near the altar and large basketfuls along the walls and aisles and in various niches. It smelled of spring, intoxicating, almost erotic.

Taking charge, Dr. Black designated Neal to be best man and told Jim that he would give the bride away. Jack was enlisted as maid of honor. Organ music wafted softly over us and then swelled abruptly as Dr. Black disappeared, giving me the chance to examine the robust woman at the organ who was swaying ecstatically with each note she produced. She was playing Bach expertly and watching us with apparent delight.

When Dr. Black returned, he was resplendent in glittering priestly vestments. Swinging incense, he led our little group to the altar. There he asked if we had brought rings. We had. We had that day bought old, broad, clunky rings from a pawnshop. As a present, the pawnshop owner asked the jeweler next door to engrave them for us, and we had chosen words from the beginning and ending of Shakespeare's sonnet number 116, which begins: "Let me not to the marriage of true minds admit impediment."

Dr. Black placed the rings in the crevice of his Bible or prayer book and held them in front of a gold cross at the altar. Daniel whispered that he was blessing the rings, and I stole another look at the organist, wondering if she was the Mrs. Black who had inspired so much lusty pleasure.

When Dr. Black faced us again, the music stopped as abruptly as it had begun, but two censers continued to leak perfumed smoke. He cleared his throat and began to read the wedding service in a strong, clear baritone. Soon he came to a series of questions, beginning "Daniel, wilt thou have this woman to be thy wedded wife," and so on. At the appropriate point, Daniel answered, "I will."

Dr. Black then turned to me with similar questions, and I was by then half-hypnotized by his sonorous phrases, the incense, and the perfume of so many flowers. I awakened suddenly from my rapture when I realized that I was being asked if I would promise to obey my husband.

"Excuse me, please," I interrupted, startling myself as well as Dr. Black, "but I cannot promise to obey."

Dr. Black stopped talking and looked at me in stern disbelief. Daniel opened his yellow eyes wider and our friends stepped closer to see if they had heard correctly. "I don't want to make promises that I know I can't keep," I explained. "Daniel is my partner, not my father."

I felt embarrassed and apologetic, but certain that I couldn't make such a pledge, not even as a ceremonial gesture. Dr. Black harrumphed and then stroked his mouth as if to erase the sound. A discussion ensued. Jack took the position that the vow was merely a ritual, a tradition that nobody took seriously. Dr. Black and Jim, a veteran attorney, disagreed. Jim said the idea of wifely obedience was incorporated in the common law of England and the Constitution of the United States, and hadn't been repealed by the Nineteenth Amendment giving women the right to vote. Dr. Black said it was a part of church doctrine, but that disobedience to a man was not itself a sin. He asked Daniel what he thought. Daniel replied that freedom of the mind was essential to our union and that he didn't ask for or want obedience.

Without telling us his decision, Dr. Black asked us to resume our places, then he began the service again, starting with the questions to Daniel. We listened intently and when it came my turn to make promises, I braced to object. But there was no need. The offensive word was not mentioned, and we were wed.

When he concluded, Dr. Black claimed the right to be the first to kiss the bride. He then produced a bottle of brandy and poured each of us a generous amount in crystal glasses brought by the organist, whose identity remained a mystery. After several toasts, we returned to Washington where we shared a final bottle of champagne and recounted Dr. Black's astonishing sex lecture to our three friends.

And we were lusty. In time we even procreated, and rather splendidly we thought. On the first day of spring, exactly two years after the wedding, we were driving through the Maryland countryside in our first car, with our infant son in a basket in the back seat, when we both had the idea to drop in on Dr. Black to let him see how well we had followed his advice. After driving a bit longer, we found the church, which looked exactly as it did before, except that this time it shone in the light of a sunny Sunday afternoon. Daniel held our pretty baby while I knocked on the porch door, which was soon opened by a thin, humorless-looking man, somewhat older than Dr. Black. He was wearing a grim, gray knitted cardigan that seemed to suggest continual winter.

We asked to see Dr. Black and up went the man's bushy gray eyebrows, lengthening a nose that resembled Richard Nixon's. "Who?" a thin mouth demanded. "The priest," I answered. "The pastor," Daniel corrected. "Dr. Black," we said in unison.

"I'm the rector of this parish," said the cardiganed man, correcting us both, "and my name is not Black!"

Daniel asked if the Dr. Black who had been there two years earlier had moved to another church in the area, but the man said he had been the only rector at the church for the past fifteen years. Perhaps Dr. Black had filled in for him when he was ill or on vacation, Daniel suggested. The man shook his head emphatically and asked why we were looking for a Dr. Black. We explained that he had married us in this church two years ago. The rector invited us to come inside and look around, since it might have been another church. We did, but the hall tree, office, and other features were exactly as before. I remembered it well because it was the only Episcopal church I had ever been inside.

When I insisted that we had the right church but the wrong man, the rector looked thoughtful. He asked when, exactly, the wedding had taken place. I told him March 21, two years earlier, on a Saturday night. "We don't perform weddings in this church on Saturday nights," he said. "Then, it's the gardener's domain. He has the keys so he can bring in the flowers and prepare the church for Sunday morning services. I usually make parish calls and keep out of the way." The rector's manner was much less brusque as he said this.

He asked us what Dr. Black looked like, and we told him as best we could in our state of shock and confusion.

"That sounds like the man we had as gardener and custodian around two years ago," he said, "but he left us that spring as I recall." We just stood there, mute, for almost a minute, digesting his words.

"I'm afraid a terrible mistake has been made," the rector said. "I fear the gardener committed an unpardonable offense."

The rector said that he would be glad to marry us himself to help right the wrong done to us. There would be no charge, he said. Indeed, he seemed most eager to see us wed. Daniel and I looked at each other over the golden head of our son, who was grinning and pawing the air. "Thank you very much," we said, "but no thank you."

The rector looked truly distressed.

"We're happy the way we are," we both explained.

Chapter Four

In the Wind

The day before Senator John F. Kennedy was inaugurated as president of the United States, the nation's capital was pasted by a late afternoon snow that anywhere else would merely have slowed traffic. Accustomed to the city's pathetic response to winter storms, most workers left their offices two hours early, looking forward to having the next day off to watch the young president and his pretty wife enter the White House through a door opened by some shady characters from Chicago. Just about everyone was delighted that the young Irish-American president had bested "Tricky Dick" Nixon, the sourpuss disciple of the late, unlamented Senator Joe McCarthy.

As usually happened when snow fell, traffic lights stopped working. And on this inauguration eve, almost all DC policemen were serving as personal escorts for political VIPs. So the city was quickly paralyzed by gridlock. After leaving his office, Daniel was unable to travel more than three blocks in six hours, during which time he listened to innumerable news accounts of the difficulties Frank Sinatra was having making the scene on a special train. City traffic remained stymied until nearly eight o'clock, when individual drivers got out of their cars, ignored the flying snow, and began to clear the clogged intersections of me-first commuters. It was a fitting end to the beat era. Although we didn't realize it, before another day would pass, passivity would become passé and deference to authority would begin a slow march over the edge of a cliff.

The next afternoon, as the glazed dome of the Capitol reflected sunlight so clear it seemed to have been distilled, the newly inaugurated president exhorted Americans to stop looking to their country for help, but to ask what they could do to help it. He encouraged bold thinking by announcing that he would trump Russia's *Sputnik* by landing an American on the moon, adding that he would never negotiate from fear but would never fear to negotiate. With such rhetorical flourishes, many of the frustrations of the fifties were swept into sixties' streets, where people would express their dissatisfactions and demands in unprecedented numbers.

Kennedy hadn't intended to encourage protest and civil discord, but the era of do-it-yourself activism was already underway when his call to action was heard by those who saw America as a white lie, as well as those who wanted to make it the light of the world. While he had been campaigning across the country, groups of students at black colleges had been studying ways to scuttle segregation. Some protesters had adapted Gandhi's tactic of civil disobedience by staging sit-ins at segregated facilities, and many had landed in jail for doing so. Integrated groups of adults had also been studying and testing ways to confront racial discrimination, while youths who had glimpsed during the Korean "police action" what the old order might do to them were primed to try almost anything to keep from becoming cannon fodder in another bungled war far from home.

In DC the most militant civil rights group during the early sixties was the local chapter of the Congress of Racial Equality (CORE). DC CORE had forty to fifty African American members and roughly the same number of whites. One reason it had a reputation for militancy was because it helped to launch the daring "Freedom Rides," which challenged segregation on interstate buses by sending racially integrated groups of riders from Washington into the Deep South. The extreme violence encountered by these "Freedom Riders" and the riders' courage in continuing despite repeated assaults rocked the nation and set a new standard of selflessness in resisting Jim Crow. Another reason for DC CORE's reputation was its black leader's penchant for projects that drove whites up the wall, as when he threatened to release live rats into white neighborhoods unless the city waged an anti-rat campaign in black neighborhoods. CORE members had in fact trapped a number of rats and sometimes, although not that time, carried out a threat to break the law nonviolently—a tactic we referred to as "civil disobedience." But most of CORE's protests—we called them "direct actions"—consisted of perfectly lawful picketing, which might be combined with civil disobedience by some members. In every case, members were trained and pledged to remain nonviolent no matter how violent law enforcement or angry opponents or bystanders became.

One very visible and tightly organized opponent was the American Nazi Party, which frequently staged counter-demonstrations and sometimes directed its storm troopers to throw eggs or rocks at CORE members in an attempt to provoke a reaction that would lead to arrests. On one such occasion, a Nazi egg landed at the feet of my mother, who had come from California to visit us, and she broke ranks and walked swiftly toward the Nazi line. Daniel and I caught up with her before the police did, and with the help of another CORE member, we succeeded in getting her back to our side of the street, where she continued to vent her anger (in three languages) with such vehemence that we had to take her home.

Whether the Nazis were present or not, the DC police used various tactics to discourage civil rights protesters, such as confronting us with police dogs, photographing each protester individually, letting us know they had investigated our private lives, rough treatment during arrests, and putting nonviolent demonstrators in jail cells with violent criminals. But for the most part, DC cops treated protesters far better than the authorities did in most southern jurisdictions.

The National Association for the Advancement of Colored People (NAACP), the senior civil rights organization, owed much of its success to its legal arm and disliked violating the law, insisting that the courtroom was the appropriate place to do battle. Under the leadership of local executive director Edward (Ed) Hailes, it participated in most civil rights campaigns that did not guarantee its members would end up in jail. The local arm of the National Urban League, led by Reverend Sterling Tucker, practiced friendly and indignant persuasion, as did the local branch of the Southern Christian Leadership Coalition (SCLC) although its activist leader, Reverend Walter Fauntroy, joined Martin Luther King, Jr., in various acts of civil disobedience in the South.

A new organization, the Student Nonviolent Coordinating Committee (SNCC), quickly took a leading role in the movement by joining in the 1961 Freedom Rides and taking on the dangerous task of registering blacks to vote in Mississippi and other Deep South states. SNCC didn't have memberships, but a courageous fistful of students at Howard University, including Stokely Carmichael, Courtland Cox, Ed Brown, and Dion Diamond, abandoned their classrooms to work (for $10 a week) as SNCC field secretaries. SNCC activists at Howard who wanted to challenge discrimination in DC usually did so through the newly formed Nonviolent Action Group (NAG). In 1965, Marion Barry, who had been SNCC's first chairman, was assigned to run SNCC's office in DC, and after the city obtained a measure of home rule, he was elected and served four terms as mayor.

DC CORE's chairman, Julius Hobson, looked and talked like a bourgeois college professor with a deep tan. He usually wore a porkpie hat with a tweed jacket over a conservative tie, and often had a pipe in his mouth at a slight angle, occasionally removing it to lecture or point at a follower, rival, or adversary. A government economist with a manner that was both thoughtful and forceful, he was quick-witted, autocratic, and confident that he could win any debate without raising his voice. When he talked about racism, he reminded me of my father; but to Washington's white press, he was a fire-breathing radical. He obviously enjoyed that image and burnished it by such tactics as threatening to release ghetto rats in Georgetown, the Washington neighborhood where many of the nation's most prominent families had homes. It was the sort of threat that outraged some but endeared him to many, and eventually produced broader attempts to reduce the rat population.

The campaign against rats was not completely atypical of DC CORE actions. Several had a highly emotional component, such as protests against police brutality and protests that spurred counter-protests by the American Nazi Party. At times the innocent members of the public might be inconvenienced, as when CORE impeded traffic along a federal highway after learning that business along the route could refuse to accommodate African Americans but must serve African diplomats and their staffs. All actions were subject to the constraints of the national CORE organization's thirteen Rules for Action, which included careful investigations; democratic procedures; a sincere effort to avoid malice or hatred; flexibility; submission to assault without retaliation; and submission to arrest without resistance. Such rules led to endless debates by members over whether every prerequisite for direct action had been met. We also had difficulty deciding which of the many practitioners of racial discrimination to attack next. Schools, hospitals, banks, hotels, bus lines, restaurants, stores, apartment buildings, and components of federal and local government were among the many culprits methodically pursued in strict compliance with the Rules for Action by the middle-class idealists in DC CORE. At first Daniel and I participated in actions as non-members, trying to avoid the internal squabbling that accompanied almost every decision—Chairman Hobson once exclaimed that it was impossible to run a revolution on *Robert's Rules of Order*—but fairly soon we were fully engaged as members.

One action that backfired on me was the Washington Hospital Center's agreement to integrate all facilities in response to CORE's picketing. I was not aware weeks later that the hospital had not been completely integrated when our son was born there on a busy Sunday morning. Because he was born by way of a Caesarian section and there was no empty incubator in the "white nursery," the surgery nurse put him in the "colored nursery." But the nursery nurses didn't think to look for him there, and so I didn't see him until the following Thursday, by which time I thought he had died.

Some of the actions undertaken by DC CORE had a complex backstory unknown by the public; for example, when CORE created public disturbances in cahoots with the DC commissioners to give them an excuse to exercise their "police powers." We would create a ruckus by blocking traffic or staging a sit-in at a place that excluded blacks, and the commissioners would ban such discrimination as a threat to public safety. However, such collaboration was rare, and I wasn't privy to any secret negotiations with commissioners, or later with elected mayors. But all CORE members were aware that as long as we lacked voting representation in Congress, no local government could do more than its congressional overseers would allow.

Despite such constraints, CORE in 1963 made creative use of a new but toothless ban on housing discrimination in DC by simultaneously ending that injustice at an apartment complex and providing a public-safety justification for a ban with enforceable penalties. After weeks of fruitless picketing, coupled with a sit-in that produced arrests, the owner capitulated when we picketed his suburban home on a Sunday morning. He not only stopped discriminating, he declined to press charges against Daniel and two others who had been arrested at the sit-in. Despite this settlement, the US Attorney for the District of Columbia attempted to discourage civil disobedience by threatening, via the *Washington Post,* to prosecute Daniel and the two others anyway. Fortunately, he was dissuaded from carrying out this threat. Unfortunately, according to a Civil Rights Commission study in 2011, neither the actions of DC government nor the broad federal ban on housing discrimination enacted in 1968 have been effective in halting such discrimination.

One unexpected pleasure that developed in the course of CORE's 1963 protest was getting to spend time with Harry Belafonte, who was performing in DC at the time. Because the local press was ignoring our picket line—it hypocritically turned a blind eye to local protests while reporting and roundly criticizing discrimination elsewhere—someone in CORE had the bright idea of inviting the famous singer, actor, and civil rights stalwart to join the line; and I and a young woman who had been arrested with Daniel a few days earlier were assigned to extend the invitation. Belafonte didn't join the line, but almost every night after his performance, sometimes without changing or removing his makeup, he came to our home where we talked and talked and talked about the movement. He knew most key players and their thinking, having served as a unique personal bridge between the Kennedys and rights leaders, including Martin Luther King, Jr., and young firebrands in SNCC and CORE. Often other friends were present, but sometimes it was just the three of us. We talked and sometimes argued about such things as King's capitulation to White House pressure to fire Jack O'Dell, who directed SCLC's automated solicitations of funds. Daniel believed that Belafonte came back night after night because, as much as I admired his civil rights activism, I was immune to what I viewed as an excess of masculine charm. One day he phoned after his theater engagement ended and asked me to go with him to his Caribbean island; I said I would ask Daniel if he minded. Daniel said I would have to take our infant son, Danny, and dog, Orfeo. And Harry said he would arrange for a nanny and a kennel. At that, the three of us laughed, and laughed some more, and then finally we said goodbye.

As the seat of the federal government, DC frequently served as a gigantic stage for rights activism throughout the sixties—and many of those who played leading roles came back several times, a large number staying to work for a while. Like other spear-carriers, Daniel and I had memorable encounters and sometimes formed lasting relationships with truly inspiring people. Belafonte was not the only star or future star to sometimes hang out at our place, where partying that combined serious scheming with music and dancing seemed to develop without planning every few days or so. It was an exciting time and not just because of the sometimes shocking events in many American cities and towns, or because big issues of war, peace, civil rights, hunger, outer space, even nuclear annihilation were on everyone's table. It was exciting because of the widely-shared sense that somehow, against great odds, we the people could bring about significant changes in the way America and the rest of the world worked.

One of our first DC friends would become a friend for life and in time an American icon. Martin Puryear was then a fine arts student at Catholic University and was in fact a treasure trove of friendships as we got to know and love his family. He was also a part-time worker at a nearby library, and a librarian there whom I had met in New York had two paintings by Martin hanging on the wall of his DC apartment. They were traditional but revealing of a promising talent, and I admired both. This prompted Ray Elgin, the librarian who had the paintings and who also became a lifetime friend, to arrange for us to meet the young artist. Soon after our meeting, Martin became a frequent visitor and quiet-speaking participant in our vigorous discussions of civil rights and cultural change, and our lives became permanently entwined. After completing a year in Sierra Leone as a Peace Corps volunteer, a course Daniel and I had encouraged, Martin scaled the artistic heights, arriving at the summit in 1989 as America's sole representative and the grand prize winner of an important international competition to select the world's current best sculptor: The São Paulo (Brazil) Bienal.

Sometime in late 1962, Daniel and I met another young man with whom we would share a close, lifelong friendship, although most of the time we would be thousands of miles apart. We met by chance and were drawn together by shared interests and values, bonding irrevocably while sharing experiences that were unusually interesting and often fun, but all-too-often shattering. Thelton Henderson had come to DC as a recent graduate of UC Berkeley's law school to work in the Civil Rights Division of Robert Kennedy's Justice Department. As the only black attorney in that division, he was frequently sent south—first to examine voter registration documents in Louisiana, and soon after to serve as the division's point-man or troubleshooter in black communities of cities and towns where conditions were (sometimes literally) explosive. For example: During the first week of May 1963, the attention of the nation and much of the world was captivated by an epic civil rights battle being waged in Alabama's largest city, Birmingham, a.k.a. Bombingham. It earned that nickname because of the large number of bombings by the Ku Klux Klan to terrorize black neighborhoods and discourage agitation for equal rights. Thelton was there for most of April, monitoring a well-organized campaign led by Martin Luther King, Jr., to protest segregation and improve employment opportunities for African Americans. Despite protest marches by thousands of black adults and the jailing of Dr. King and many others, the national press paid little attention, and the campaign appeared to be failing, until on May 2 a stream of children began to flow out of the Sixteenth Street Baptist Church. One by one close to a thousand children exited the church, cut though an adjacent park, and walked single file down one of Birmingham's main streets, singing, smiling, and carrying signs that demanded "FREEDOM" and "EQUALITY" and other rights that were supposed to be theirs at birth. They continued to walk with heads high until they made history as the largest group of American children ever to be arrested at one time.

The next day, with the Birmingham jails still crammed with children, another church-full of youthful protesters walked purposefully along the same route and into an ambush by a combat force that might have given General Ulysses S. Grant pause. Waiting to attack them were hundreds of policemen wearing pistols and brandishing shotguns or riot guns, truncheons, cattle prods, and other weapons. They were accompanied by batteries of firemen with high-velocity water hoses and police canine squads with German Shepherds straining at their leashes. When the children refused to turn back, Public Safety Commissioner Eugene "Bull" Connor gave the order to attack them with truncheons, dogs, and water. The chaos that followed was captured by television and newspaper photographers and promptly reported around the globe. Conscious of the damage to America's image abroad, the Kennedys, like millions of others, were especially upset by images of children being set upon by police dogs, of children knocked down, pinned against walls, pummeled, and propelled head-over-heels by water from firemen's hoses, and of terrified children being forcibly arrested by armed and helmeted patrolmen.

In the week that followed, protests continued and the police, bolstered by five hundred state troopers sent by newly elected Governor George Wallace, continued to abuse protesters on camera. As a go-between for rights leaders and the Justice Department, Thelton warned the former that they should not tell him anything they didn't want to get back to the latter, and he did his best to keep personal feelings at bay. He attended most of the civil rights rallies in African American churches, where the music and oratory rocked the structure almost enough to flatten walls or topple a steeple. At times he was the only public official present during debates within the civil rights community on such highly emotional issues as whether to expose children to arrest. His reports went quickly up the chain of command at the Justice Department and into the White House, where a very troubled president wrestled with the question of what to do. Reluctant to send troops or federal marshals to Birmingham, he sent Burke Marshall, who commanded the Justice Department's Civil Rights Division, and used back-channels to get Birmingham's industrial overlords to persuade local department stores to integrate lunch counters, water fountains, and fitting rooms, and improve employment opportunities for African Americans. The white business leaders also agreed to participate in a biracial committee to consider further steps to dismantle segregation. Within hours of the agreement that was supposed to restore calm and end the tarnishing of America's image abroad, the Birmingham home of Martin Luther King, Jr.'s brother, A. D. King, was bombed, as was the A. G. Gaston Motel, where MLK and his lieutenants stayed, as did Thelton.

The anger generated by these bombings threatened to explode at any moment from random acts of violence into a full-scale riot. At times Thelton was about the only person officially connected with law enforcement that a black witness or victim would talk to. So many bombs had been exploded earlier in a black neighborhood where a civil rights lawyer lived that it was known throughout the city as Dynamite Hill. A bomb would explode and several minutes later a second bomb would. The second one would be filled with nails and other shrapnel, and when it detonated, it would rip the flesh of the residents who had gathered to help the first victims. Thelton interviewed a man who said he had seen policemen plant bombs and return after two explosions and pretend to investigate. The police insisted the man wasn't credible and the FBI agreed. Whether he was or not, the Bureau for forty years concealed the identity of members of the Klan's bombing crew because one of them had been one of their informers. To say the least, such behavior made it difficult and even dangerous for Bombingham's genuine, well-intentioned responders to do their jobs after Klan terror attacks.

Less than a month later, Thelton was sent by the Justice Department to Jackson, Mississippi immediately after the assassination of Medgar

Evers, an NAACP leader revered in the movement for his cool courage and tenacity in attacking racial injustice. After the funeral, which was attended by thousands of people, Thelton accompanied a group of youths who deviated from the route through Jackson prescribed by the police and were confronted by a wall of police armed with shotguns and rifles. When a few of the youths responded with rocks and bottles, the police raised their guns and aimed to fire. At that moment Thelton's supervisor, John Doar, broke through the police line and, standing between the two groups, persuaded the youths to disburse. For preventing a slaughter, Doar received a Presidential Medal plus our profound thanks for sparing Thelton a severe case of lead poisoning from police gunfire.

While Thelton was being transferred from one crisis to another across the Southeast, Daniel and I were desperately trying to prevent the execution of a friend of his from California who had been staying at Thelton's Washington apartment while recuperating from an accident. The friend, whom I'll call Ben, had also stayed with us, and we both thought that he was one of the most genuinely gentle, considerate, and well-meaning people we had ever known. He was also gracefully athletic—such an expert diver that the young white adults at Thelton's apartment complex were drawn to him and included him in some of their social activities. And he was so all-over attractive that one of the white women took him as her lover. Unfortunately, she came to believe that she was pregnant and that the only way she could get a legal abortion was to charge a black man with rape. So, after having sex, she bit Ben's face hard enough to raise an ugly welt and ran down the corridor of the apartment building virtually naked and yelling for help.

At the preliminary hearing the next morning, Ben amazed his temporary court-appointed lawyer by telling him not to further upset the woman who had accused him of a crime for which he almost certainly would be hanged if convicted. There was reason to fear that he might not make it to trial, since he was denied bail and DC jail at that time was run mainly by white southern men with traditional views. Put in a cell with a powerful sexual predator, Ben kept from being raped by staying awake and upright until he was able to start a fight that landed him in solitary confinement. He managed to stay there for many months, and then got transferred to Saint Elizabeth's Hospital for evaluation of his mental competence to stand trial.

While Ben was incarcerated, Daniel and I tried unsuccessfully to get rights groups to defend him—"if he's convicted, we'll help with the appeal," was the best response—and I then tried to work with the labor-law firm appointed to defend him. I was surprised by the choice, but Daniel explained that, for DC capital cases, defense attorneys are appointed without regard to their specialty or experience. One lawyer at the firm had prior trial experience, but as a prosecutor, and everyone there apparently thought that the bloody bite and naked flight down the hallway signified a badly wronged woman. I must have sounded terribly naive to these white attorneys when I insisted over and over again that Ben would never have harmed any woman of any hue, that he was absolutely incapable of rape, and that his refusal to let his arraignment lawyer say anything that might upset his accuser was proof of his unalterable gentleness and respect for the feelings of others. I offered to take a lie detector test and testify under oath that Ben would severely injure himself rather than have sex with a woman who said no. I even pointed out that my survival during the Holocaust had depended on distinguishing between good and evil men, and that my extensive experience with the latter had taught me how to tell the difference.

The former prosecutor's skeptical look didn't vanish when I told him this, but he said he would interview the young people in the apartment complex who knew both Ben and his accuser. When we talked weeks later, however, he said that the young people were not only solidly behind the woman, they were so angry with Ben that they wanted to hang him themselves for impregnating their friend and forcing her to seek an abortion. They had also demanded that the building owners evict Thelton Henderson for letting Ben stay in his apartment, he added, looking progressively more puzzled as my smile grew wider and wider.

"If she's pregnant," I said, realizing what was behind the rape accusation, "Ben is not the father!" I explained that Ben had undergone a vasectomy at his wife's request so they wouldn't have more children, and she had later taken their children and left him for someone else. Understandably, Ben had been severely shaken, and had subsequently experienced a solo accident that friends feared had been an attempt to self-destruct. Normally poker-faced, the lawyer sat back in his chair, took a deep breath that resembled a sigh, then cracked a smile that for a change was not faintly condescending. He said this would help the case and that there was more he knew that could. He said that the night clerk at Thelton's building had seen Ben and the young woman take the elevator to Thelton's floor many nights, and she had not returned to the ground floor until morning. If this was the case, the woman was clearly spending time with Ben because she wanted to, not because she was raped. He said this statement did not mean Ben was in the clear—the prosecution's case was still formidable, but he now had tools to work with. Several weeks later he called to say that they had pursued these leads and found that the night clerk, who was white, was willing to testify in court; that Ben had finally admitted the affair and the vasectomy; and that the accuser was not and had not been pregnant. But she didn't change her claim of being raped when this was found out. The lawyer said that the firm wanted to take the highly unusual step of laying out the facts in advance to the trial judge, a Virginian reputed to be traditional but fair, and who had interrupted his retirement to try the case. The prosecutor, who had probably arranged to get a "hanging judge," promised that he wouldn't oppose a motion to dismiss if the proffered evidence of Ben's innocence was truly persuasive. Ben had said okay even though he had been warned that his defense would be a lot more difficult if the judge refused to dismiss and the case went to trial. Ben's lawyer wanted to know if Thelton, Daniel, and I approved. We did. Soon after, the judge dismissed the charge, and ten days later Daniel and I picked up Ben at the gate to the DC jail. We made him keep his head down until we were safely out of DC and (we hoped safely) inside our home in suburban Maryland. The next morning I put him on a plane to California.

Chapter Five

Grand March

Two-and-a-half halcyon years after the Kennedys came into power, an unstructured but vibrant civil rights movement was poised to stage a massive march, the March on Washington for Jobs and Freedom. During the weeks leading up to the march, I worked as a volunteer organizer, working first in hastily rented DC offices and later in a tent on the mall between the Capitol building and the Lincoln Memorial. I spent most of my time on the phone, persuading people and organizations to participate, answering all sorts of questions about transportation, lodging, and the program, and helping to distribute hastily prepared informational pamphlets. The march was opposed at first by the Kennedys, who had spoken eloquently about the injustices fueling "Negro" discontent and had even sent a civil rights bill to Congress, but who had given some people the impression that they were motivated more by a desire to protect America's image than by a determination to change the racial status quo. In any case, the Kennedys dropped their opposition to the march after its leaders included support for the bill in their agenda.

Needless to say, the march was a subject that generated controversy within and outside the civil rights movement, with many people saying it would be untimely, unpatriotic, and probably violent, while others feared it would be a flop for lack of attendance. Those of us working to make the march a success were eager to know what was being said about it in the press. As a lower-level volunteer, I only fielded perfunctory press inquiries, but Daniel and I knew many journalists since he was a writer and editor for large publishers, first in New York and later in DC, where he also served as chairman of the Newspaper Guild Bargaining Unit at the employee-owned company. He also served on the governing board of the huge Washington Newspaper Guild, and I went with him to Guild functions, including picket lines. Soon after the march was announced, he volunteered to coordinate Guild participation in it. So we were fairly well attuned to reporters' attitudes.

Unfortunately, the fourth estate was almost as rigidly segregated in the North as in the South, where even some black publications with a conservative bent were hostile to the march. The main bastions of northern liberalism, the *Washington Post* and the *New York Times*, had no black reporters and the national TV networks had, at maximum, one black correspondent or anchorman. For the most part, though, the national white press did a creditable and sometimes courageous job covering protests in the South. But northern publishers and editorial boards were far less sanguine about hometown expressions of discontent, and DC was to some extent every national news organization's hometown.

The national black press, which included the *Pittsburgh Courier* and the *Afro-American* newspapers in many cities, and widely-read magazines such as *Negro Digest*, *Ebony*, and *Jet*, devoted considerable space to black reluctance or opposition—notably Malcolm X's haughty put-down when he predicted it would be a "Farce" rather than a "March" on Washington. The civil rights organizations that supported the march had very different approaches and competed fiercely for prestige and revenues. Some of the leaders wouldn't speak to each other except in public, and national CORE National Director James Farmer elected to sit out the march in a

Louisiana jail and let the national chairman take his place. Religious leaders had difficulty making up their minds and labor unions were divided, with some international unions, such as the United Auto Workers (UAW), giving critical support while others prevented the executive committee of the American Federation of Labor-Congress of Industrial Organizations (AFL-CIO) from endorsing the march. In striking contrast, a national group of Catholic bishops gave it their blessing, although a key archbishop later threatened to withdraw unless the SNCC spokesman, John Lewis, agreed to tone down criticism of the Kennedy administration. While it reported the noisy discord preceding the march, the national black press clearly saw the need to take a stand on the steps of the Lincoln Memorial against America's enduring racism. Daniel thought the scornful criticism of the march by Malcolm X, a spokesman for the Nation of Islam, might have been elicited by the march's chief organizer and deputy director, Bayard Rustin, to get hesitant Christian leaders to step forward. Whether that was the case or not, after Malcolm X called the march a farce, some church leaders who hadn't endorsed the march immediately did so.

While most of the journalists that Daniel and I talked with were sympathetic to the march's general aims, such as greater access to jobs and the ballot box, and thought it would be a peaceful protest with the religious community heavily involved, their editors appeared to be increasingly anxious about the prospect of a large number of angry African Americans marching in DC. As August 28 drew closer, the potential for violence was examined from every conceivable angle, with reporters demanding to know what routes would be taken, what measures would be in place to maintain order, and what resources would be brought to bear if the peace was broken. Since most whites thought CORE members were troublemakers, the fact that DC CORE's fittest would be serving as marshals wasn't reassuring. In the last days before the march, the white press's concern for public safety seemed almost obsessive to march workers. Even the *New York Times* speculated on the possibility that marchers might become violent.

The unkindest cut of all was the *Washington Post*'s personal attack on Bayard Rustin. The *Post* painted him as a sexual deviant with a criminal record and a communist past that raised serious questions about what would happen on August 28. A Gandhi disciple who was openly socialist and privately gay, Rustin had demonstrated the courage of his nonviolent convictions by going to jail numerous times to extend the blessings of democracy to all Americans. Fortunately, he refused to give his African American scalp to the *Washington Post*, which unfortunately continued to discourage participation in the march by warnings of possible violence. If the *Washington Post* ever endorsed the march, its statement of support was too late and too limited to affect the fears it had created of black violence. Many black as well as white Washingtonians stayed home because of what they read and heard, which explains why DC participation was lower than that of some other cities and helps to explain why whites were only about twenty percent of the march total, even though white religious leaders, entertainers, and celebrities were prominently in the forefront.

At the march's headquarters, we were not as worried that some marchers might attack white persons or white-owned businesses—the clear focus of the media's concern—as we were that the increasingly widespread violence against African Americans would deter too many people from participating. News photos and accounts of violent attacks on blacks by mobs and police throughout the South were still vivid in the minds of many people. Such savagery, plus dire press reports, threats by racist organizations and public officials, and planted rumors, made it difficult for us to obtain buses and drivers, especially in the Deep South. Filling those buses was not quite as difficult, although it required individual acts of courage by people who lived with the knowledge that even the slightest affront to a white person could cost them dearly.

Sitting in the large information tent near the Washington Monument around 4:00 a.m. on the morning of August 28, 1963, I was tired but wide awake and beginning to be apprehensive about the buses that hadn't arrived from the Deep South. The march organizers had prepared as best they could for around 100,000 marchers, but those of us who were there to greet marchers and tell them where to go had no way of knowing how many would show up or what the racial mix might be. Although no one said so, the fear that at least some of the buses had been intercepted or attacked was evident in the facial expressions of coworkers. I tried not to finger the beautiful orchid lei from Hawaii that had been placed around my neck a couple of hours earlier by Lena Horne. She had set us aglow with encouragement by coming to see us and showing her support and then turning as she left and singing out to all of us, "You are beautiful!"

As time passed and only a few visitors arrived, several of the workers departed, leaving only six of us—three men and three women. Around 4:30, a photographer came inside and asked to take our pictures with his Polaroid camera. I posed, sitting on the knee of my favorite march worker, Ed Brown, who represented SNCC on the DC Leadership Committee. Ed was studying economics at Howard University and I had been helping him translate Karl Marx from German into English. After the photographer departed, Ed tried to cheer us both up by recounting one of the escapades of his younger brother, Herbert, nicknamed "Rap" because of his acerbic wit and gift for sustained, sometimes rhymed verbal acrobatics. But all conversation stopped and all of us sprang to our feet when someone stuck his head into the tent and said that the first bus had arrived from Mississippi. Sighs of relief turned into joyful smiles and even a little impromptu dancing.

One volunteer stayed in the tent while the rest of us ran quickly to the parking area where the passengers were milling about, trying to get a clear view of the White House in the distance and the Washington Monument poking up behind our tent.

"Welcome! Welcome to the March on Washington!" Ed said loudly in his rich baritone.

"We are so glad to see you!" a coworker repeated breathlessly several times. I added my own welcome, shook many hands, and embraced several people whose smiles suggested they might have been almost as happy to see me as I was to see them. The orchids suffered, but I didn't care.

"How many will you be?" Ed asked.

"There should be at least three hundred of us," said a stout man with a silver mustache and a clerical collar. "But, you know, we could have lost some along the way if their bus broke down or was stopped by police or the Klan."

We formed a circle with the passengers and bowed our heads while the clergyman led us in a prayer of thanks for the safe trip, to which Ed and I and everybody else said amen. Then we joined hands and sang "We Shall Overcome." At least the others sang. I started off well enough but soon choked up listening to the refrain: "We shall build a new world! We shall build a new world some day!"

Their voices weren't the only emotional stimulant. While they sang, one bus after another rolled into the parking area and stopped with a hiss of airbrakes. After surveying the dark faces peering out of open bus windows and exiting gingerly through the opened doors, Ed stopped singing for a moment, leaned close to me, and joyfully exclaimed in my ear, "It's going to be a Nigger march after all!"

Many hours later, I listened to a loudspeaker pour out Martin Luther King, Jr.'s dream of an America in which people would be judged by the content of their character rather than the color of their skin, while Daniel watched and listened from a grassy ridge near the Lincoln Memorial. It was a wonderful, and at times magical, day. It was hot and it was humid, as Washington is in late August; the water supply was inadequate, and some marchers suffered from the shortage while thousands splashed their legs like bathing beauties in the reflecting pool. But it was neither too hot nor too humid, and there was a slight breeze that wandered among the attentive listeners, helped along by those with fans. The real warmth though was the good will that strangers had for one another, so palpable and healing that everyone felt its presence as if another element had been added to earth, air, fire, and water.

After Martin Luther King, Jr., shared his iconic "I have a dream" speech, bestowing his blessing on the entire world for as long as time is kept, all of us sensed that we had participated in one of the most glorious civic events ever. It was an unprecedented gathering of people of goodwill to demand an end to centuries of racial oppression. It was also the most peaceful day on record for the nation's capital. Along with many other people who witnessed it on TV, the Kennedys apparently were impressed. In the Oval Office, immediately after the march, the president promised the march leaders that he would push the civil rights bill then languishing on Capitol Hill. (Jack and Jacqueline later invited Martin and Coretta to lunch.) The next day, however, the *Post* printed what I remember as an almost full-page photo of the litter, mostly abandoned placards, left on the mall.

The months after the magnificent march were even more traumatic for believers in democracy and human rights than those leading up to it For reasons we didn't understand, the Justice Department, with little justification, sent Thelton out of town shortly before the march. Given the size of the event and the media's and city's fears of widespread violence—schools and shops near the severely restricted march area were told to close and take precautions—it didn't make sense to exile the Civil Rights Division's only black attorney at a time when he might be needed as a troubleshooter and communications link to black leaders. We wondered why they'd done this, but couldn't come up with a good answer. Fifty years later it would be revealed that the department had secretly tapped into the sound and video transmission equipment used at the march, so that it could monitor every public speaker and shut the system down whenever it chose. When I learned this, I thought it likely that J. Edgar Hoover, who knew that Thelton had a friendly relationship with King and other rights leaders, had not wanted Thelton to be anywhere near their surveillance project.

After Ben's ordeal and departure from Washington, Thelton's apartment was usually empty, and Thelton didn't want to live there anyway. At our invitation he moved in with Daniel and me, our two-year-old son, Danny, and our two-year-old black standard poodle, Orfeo. We lived in a modest rented house on a quiet lane in Montgomery County, Maryland, two blocks past the street that served as the boundary between Maryland and the District of Columbia. Three weeks after the march, Thelton was returning home from a trip south on a beautiful Sunday afternoon, when the radio beside the front door interrupted regular broadcasting to announce that an African American church in Birmingham had been bombed, resulting in a serious loss of life. Without taking off the snap-brim straw hat he wore to fend off the Dixie sun, he picked up the phone and called the Justice Department. Minutes later he was back in his used blue Volkswagen Beetle, driving as fast as he could toward Andrews Air Force Base in the southeast corner of Washington. Upon arrival, he climbed into the seat behind the pilot of an Air Force fighter jet, and little more than an hour later he was in Birmingham and on his way to the Sixteenth Street Baptist Church, which he knew well because it had been the staging area for most of the massive demonstrations that had astonished the world four months earlier. He was terribly angry and had a lump in his throat, having learned that the bombers, most likely the KKK, had targeted the children's Sunday school and had killed and injured several young girls. It made him sick to think that these were probably the same bombers who had been getting away with murder and attempted murder for years.

"The bastards did this because they knew they could get by with it," he said standing before the blasted church stones and several bystanders who were unable to hear anything but their own outrage and misery. Finally encountering someone who recognized him, he learned that most of the SCLC ministers had gone off to preach peace in black neighborhoods that were ready to explode. Hoping to catch up with the peacemakers, Thelton headed toward the frequently bombed area known as "Dynamite Hill," realizing as he neared it that he was more fearful about the reception he would get than at any time since joining Justice. Exiting his car, he felt like he was entering a Roman arena filled with snarling lions. Angry people milled about in the streets, loudly expressing their anguish and their desire to skin alive anyone connected to the bombing. No one there wanted to hear soothing words from a stranger who claimed to represent federal justice, no matter what his color. When he returned to DC more than a week later, Thelton told us that the respect SCLC leaders had earned from local blacks during the spring campaign was the only thing that prevented an incredibly bloody race war.

The murder of four girls as they were attending Sunday school raised questions that probed much deeper than the immediate ones: "Who were the killers and who let them get by with murder?" While it was impossible to know precisely what was on the killers' psychopathic minds, it seemed likely that the bombers wanted to exact revenge for the rights movement's Birmingham campaign and possibly for the participation of children in those demonstrations. Whether or not it was also a response to the March on Washington—many people thought so—was also unknown, and some questioned publicly whether the march had actually accomplished anything. Malcolm X, who had resented the Nation of Islam's refusal to avenge police killings of its members in Los Angeles and had derided the march, was looked upon by more young people as a prophet. Nonviolence was questioned inside the civil rights movement as well as by critics and bystanders who had never practiced it.

There had been many bombings prior to the march—of churches, private homes, schools, buses, and even the A. G. Gaston motel, where rights leaders and notable nonviolent advocates such as Joan

Baez stayed in Birmingham. Thelton also stayed at that motel, and on one occasion checked out only hours before a bomb exploded. The bombing of a children's Sunday school, however, had drastically elevated the level of vindictive pain that racists might inflict on innocents. It compelled rights leaders and workers to ask themselves whether they had the right to provoke such savagery. Thousands of the nation's civic and religious leaders and millions of their followers not only objected to certain tactics, such as civil disobedience or the participation of children; they opposed any protests and tolerated or sided with segregationists. As Martin Luther King, Jr., famously observed in his largely ignored letter from a Birmingham jail to prominent clergymen, for some there is never an appropriate time for protest. Even within the movement, probably a majority were opposed to civil disobedience, greatly preferring court suits and activities that were clearly protected by the Constitution. After the Sunday school bombing, the advocates for armed resistance spoke louder and many more moderate African American men asserted that they couldn't participate in protests because they couldn't trust themselves to remain nonviolent in the face of violence. Of course no one of sound mind wanted to endanger the lives of children; but after considerable soul searching, the unspoken consensus seemed to be that a retreat from confrontation would jeopardize the lives and futures of generations of children.

Bombs, police snipers, and enraged officials, onlookers, and victims were not the only hazards that Thelton had to face in the course of his duties. As a black administration official, he received special attention from police, press, members of segregationist organizations, and even elements such as the FBI within the Justice Department. He was expected to obey laws imposing racial segregation and occasionally he was abused by police who didn't recognize him as a federal official. On one such occasion, he was arrested and clubbed by a sheriff who broke the telephone connection and changed his tune when Thelton used his one phone call to contact the Justice Department and ask to speak to Attorney General Robert Kennedy.

Some of the most painful issues Thelton had to contend with were the FBI's insistence that it lacked authority to prevent violence against rights workers or voter registrants and the White House's reluctance to use troops or other protective force in the South. The Kennedys were still smarting from the charge that they had used excessive force in September 1962 to enforce a court order allowing James Meredith to become the first black to enroll in the University of Mississippi. The president had deployed units of the Mississippi National Guard when three hundred federal officials, many of them US Marshals, were unable to quell rioting by enraged whites, which had already injured scores of people and taken two lives, one a French journalist.

One of the most annoying things about Thelton's job was being called on the carpet to defend accusations of misconduct in the southern press, which was assiduously monitored and apparently taken as gospel by the FBI. Attending an integrated prayer meeting might be portrayed by the press as an attempt to formant revolution or to seduce white women. He had been forced to respond to several such distortions and fabrications that he felt should not have been taken seriously.

I was mindful of that background when Thelton called on a mid-November morning from Birmingham's Gaston Motel to tell me that he was resigning from the Justice Department and would be coming home soon. During the night he had been awakened by a phone call from a member of the department asking if he had chauffeured Martin Luther King, Jr., that day to a rally in Selma, Alabama, and had driven him from there to other events across the state. Awake but highly annoyed at yet another gross distortion, Thelton told the caller he hadn't driven King anywhere and had been in Birmingham the entire day. Asked where his car was, Thelton said it was parked in front of the motel. He woke up later that morning, nagged by the uncomfortable feeling that he should have taken the time to give the caller a fuller account of the previous day's unusual and rather complex events.

Around ten in the morning the previous day, Thelton had been approached by an SCLC pastor who was supposed to drive King to Selma for an important rally to register voters despite the sometimes violent opposition of racist thugs and Dallas County Sheriff James Clark. The pastor said that King needed to be there by noon and that he would have to drive fast, but his car had a bad front tire that could blow at any point along the way. This was particularly dangerous since King was being shadowed by racists, likely including the man who had assassinated Medgar Evers, who were looking for an opportunity to dispose of King. The pastor said King knew the threat but refused to change his course or timetable, and he implored Thelton to swap cars with him to both avoid blowing the tire and also confuse the men who were trailing King. Thelton considered the risks, and then exchanged keys.

As soon as he was fully awake, Thelton called Justice and told the whole story of the preceding day's events, apologizing for his brevity the night before. But he was too late. When the department called him earlier, it was because it had been confronted with a press report in which Alabama Governor George Wallace accused the administration of chauffeuring King around the state, stoking racial unrest everywhere they stopped. The governor claimed this proved what he had been charging all along, that the Kennedys were behind the racial turmoil that had plagued the nation since they came to power. After its quick call to Thelton, the Justice Department had issued a statement saying that Wallace's charge was an enormous fabrication, that no one connected to the Department had driven King anywhere. Wallace responded that he had proof that the car in which King had been traveling had been rented by Justice Department attorney Thelton Henderson.

As soon as he was told about the Justice Department's faulty press release, Thelton again apologized for his role in the affair, and tendered his resignation. The department issued a correcting statement, explaining that it had been unaware that an employee had allowed King's driver to borrow his rental car for a few hours. This action had not been authorized or condoned, the new release made clear, and the employee had resigned. However, the obsessed champion of "segregation forever" believed that he had harpooned the great white whale of Yankee liberalism, and he was not about to drop the line.

Endowed with unlimited chutzpah, Governor Wallace by November of 1973 had already decided to run for the office of president of the United States. As the Napoleon of an army of states-rights supremacists, he must have felt that Thelton's regard for King's safety had given him an issue he could use to evict Jack Kennedy from the White House and install, if not himself, someone of his choosing in the office. At the very least, he may have thought he could become the power broker for a box-full of electoral votes. He mounted a campaign of press attacks and political maneuvering around the theme that the Kennedy administration had been secretly sowing racial discord and harvesting violence to gain support for a second term. The "incontestable" evidence was Thelton's car rental agreement and the sworn statements of Alabama state troopers (a.k.a. Wallace's storm troopers) who had lifted the hood and taken down the registration number of the car that brought King to Selma. Very quickly it was asserted that Thelton misused government funds, contracts, property, etc., to promote insurrection and that this almost certainly amounted to serious criminal conduct that should be investigated by a special grand jury with wide-ranging authority. Not content with just the local spotlight, Wallace put in motion plans to have the grand jury flown to Washington, DC, where its actions could be monitored by press from around the world. When Thelton phoned to tell us of this almost (but not really) laughable scheme, Daniel and I said we would organize a demonstration protesting this for being a

Potemkin village grand jury—a propaganda stunt that lacked real authority.

A few days later, on November 22, Thelton was back in Washington and Wallace and Kennedy were both in Dallas, Texas. Wallace was there to hold a press conference and denounce Kennedy as unfit for office because Thelton had allowed Martin Luther King, Jr., to use his rental car. Kennedy was there to garner support for a second term. I have heard that the leader of the free world encountered his wannabe successor in the airport, but I don't know whether that is true. An hour or so later, as he was being driven down a street in Dallas, President John F. Kennedy was killed by bullets that struck with the power of nuclear fission, creating a toxic cloud of doubt and mistrust that will circle the globe for generations.

In the wake of all this, Daniel rented a television set and he and Thelton and I watched as the aftermath of the event played out in black and white, most of the time with a poignancy and dignity unmatched by classic Greek theater. But when we saw, as it was happening two days after the assassination, a man with a gun shoot and kill prime suspect Lee Harvey Oswald, who was being held by two Dallas policemen, we had the feeling we were watching the *Three Stooges* while experiencing electric shock.

Although the nation had received a wound from which it would never fully recover, the assassination of John Kennedy did not halt the civil rights movement for long. When President Lyndon B. Johnson demanded that Congress honor President Kennedy by passing the civil rights bills our slain leader had sent to them, it was, Daniel said, like a trumpet sounding reveille after last night's taps. So we got up and went back to work.

Chapter Six

The Baldwins and O'Dell

After Kennedy's death, Wallace abandoned his attempt to discredit the Kennedys by attacking Thelton, who remained a part of the Ingram household for a few more months before moving back to California to practice law and eventually becoming a Stanford Law School dean and later a federal district judge. Before he left DC, Thelton and I went to hear James Baldwin speak at Howard University. Baldwin had captured the attention of the White House and others who thought seriously about the persistence of racism in America with the essays in his book *The Fire Next Time*, one of which was published in the *New Yorker* in 1963. Daniel had also wanted to go, but our babysitter had cancelled at the last minute, so he needed to stay with our son. So after the speech I called Daniel from the auditorium to see how he and Danny were faring and to tell him how brilliant Baldwin had been.

"That's great, I'm glad to hear it," Daniel interrupted, "but I'd be a lot happier if you brought him home so I could hear him."

I told Thelton about Daniel's request and he told Baldwin, whom he had met in Mississippi at the funeral for Medgar Evers and in

Alabama after the bombing of Sixteenth Street Baptist Church. An hour after I spoke with Thelton, we surprised and delighted Daniel when we returned home with James Baldwin, his brother David, their friend Jack O'Dell, and about twenty other people passionately interested in the civil rights struggle. Thelton and several others were carrying large paper bags containing cartons of steaming food from the Peking Palace restaurant on Connecticut Avenue, which was where Daniel and I had first met Thelton more than a year earlier. Some of the visitors brought five-gallon jugs of red or white wine, and we talked and ate and talked and drank and talked and smoked and laughed until dawn. Everybody had something to say and just about everyone, including James Baldwin, seemed eager to imbibe the thoughts of others. Some, like David Baldwin, didn't talk a lot, while James talked more than any three people combined, usually in response to requests for amplification of his thoughts on people, places, and events he had written or spoken about.

James spoke passionately but thoughtfully, often pausing to contemplate or puff a cigarette before responding to a comment or question. I was drawn to him as a person as well as to his ideas because it was clear that he cared enough to think hard about almost every aspect of the human condition. Blackness mattered to him, and civil rights, but so did personal relationships, history, religion, choices, feelings, the thoughts of children, and even the taste of food. Watching him pick with chopsticks at a plate with a few Chinese dumplings on it, I was reminded that he had once questioned whether a country that didn't make decent bread could be said to have a soul. As he munched a dumpling, I told him that Germans made great bread but had no soul. He looked up, swallowed, and smiled before replying:

"Like Faust, baby, they sold it to the devil."

He was short, with a large head that made his body look even smaller than it was, and his large, slightly bulging eyes were as expressive as Joan Crawford's, but were often sad, even when he smiled. The quick, precise movements of his hands as he smoked reminded me of Bette Davis. Looking at him sit with tight knees on our living room hassock, and listening to him recall the painful realization that America had wanted him to die young in Harlem, it was obvious that he was as lonely and vulnerable as he was intellectually formidable. He had honed his critical faculties and linguistic skills to such acuity that he could defeat a William Buckley in an Oxford Union debate with the androgynous grace of a fencing master. These were the weapons that had enabled him to survive and in time transcend Harlem. But they were also weapons that could drive away lovers, and it was clear that Jimmy needed to be loved.

At one point during the night, I looked at David Baldwin to see if he was looking at his brother with love. To my surprise it was me that he was looking at, and the emotion he conveyed was clear, unfiltered yearning. I was astonished that I responded with a warm, full-bodied flush of mutual attraction. David had a mouth-circling mustache, which I didn't like, and was not much better looking than James, except that his eyes were set deeper and his skin had a dark glow. Except for Daniel, however, I had never been particularly attracted to a traditionally good-looking man, and, since Daniel, I had never felt such excitement for anyone else. I was both amazed and thrilled as David and I stared at one another for what may have been a full minute, each of us aware of what the other was going through, until Jack O'Dell broke the spell by declaring in a loud voice:

"This phone is tapped!"

Jack had just completed a call on our phone and was standing by our phone table holding the receiver in one hand.

"I don't know whether you're aware of it," he said after Daniel, Thelton, and I gave him our rapt attention, "but your phone is tapped. Believe me, I've had a lot of experience in such matters and I know what I'm talking about. I'm certain, or I wouldn't say anything."

"It's probably my fault," Thelton said, "because of the King car thing, possibly even before. Hoover was on my back practically from the first day I came to Justice."

"That could be it," O'Dell and Baldwin agreed. Daniel and I were upset, but didn't pursue the discussion because we didn't want Thelton to feel worse. Then, since it was almost light out, we began to arrange places for people to cop a few hours of sleep. I said a discreet goodnight to David and it was obvious to both of us that the intense emotions we had felt earlier had not dissipated. I tried not to say or do anything that would encourage David to think anything might come of my obvious feelings for him, but afterward I didn't think I had succeeded.

The next morning, over coffee and croissants, I learned that Jack O'Dell had been fired from his job as a fundraiser for King's Southern Christian Leadership Conference (SCLC) after the president and Robert Kennedy had twisted both of King's arms. They had done so because of J. Edgar Hoover's insistence that O'Dell was a red spy. During the McCarthy era, James Baldwin explained, Jack had refused to testify before a snoop committee headed by Senator James Eastland of Mississippi. Jack had told Eastland he wasn't a legitimate senator because blacks couldn't vote in Mississippi. Jack had also told the House of Representatives' House Un-American Activities Committee (HUAC), notorious for trying to make dissent look like treason, that he wouldn't dignify their witch-hunt by answering their questions.

Baldwin said that Hoover would probably strike again because of an article Jack had written for *Freedomways*, a journal edited by the widow of W. E. B. Du Bois, the scholar and founder of the NAACP who had joined the Communist Party not long before he died. Jack's article, Baldwin explained, was about large northern companies whose factories and subsidiaries in the South practiced racial discrimination. He wrote that the directors of some of those companies posed as liberals at home, even serving on the board of the Urban League or NAACP.

When I indicated that Daniel and I would love to read the article, Jack wrote "Compliments" on the flyleaf of his only copy, then signed it and gave it to me. He quieted my polite refusal by saying that he would be able to get another copy but that, because of the controversy surrounding it, I might have difficulty finding one.

At DC's National Airport a few hours later, Daniel and I sat with Jack and the Baldwins in the tiny cocktail lounge, sharing a bottle of champagne while waiting for their delayed flight to New York to be called. With our son sitting on his knee, James proposed a toast, predicting in a Delphic manner that Danny would one day become president of the United States. A few minutes later, after the restless three-year-old had begun to stray from the lounge area, Baldwin suddenly bolted after him, having noticed that Danny was moving rapidly toward an escalator. Daniel dashed after them but James arrived first and swooped Danny up in his arms just as Danny was about to climb onto the escalator. Seeing our blond, fair, blue-eyed boy tightly clasped in Baldwin's arms, a visibly upset, elderly white woman looked about for a policeman and loudly demanded to know:

"Is that your child?"

"Don't worry, madam," Baldwin replied, "he's mine." Smiling broadly, he carried Danny back to our table and handed him to me. Some people who had seen the incident and possibly recognized Baldwin came over to the table to compliment him on the rescue. One who definitely recognized him was Joan Fontaine, an actress who had recently starred with Harry Belafonte in a film that broke a movie taboo on interracial romance. She came to our table and after charming pleasantries made it clear that she would be interested in playing the part of the tragic heroine in a film version of Baldwin's latest novel, *Another Country*. James said he wasn't sure when that would be produced, but that he would soon be casting a new play called *Blues for Mr. Charlie*. He explained that "Mr. Charlie" was the name many black people in the South used when referring to a white landowner. Before she left, Joan Fontaine told James that she and many others greatly admired his civil rights activities as well as his literary works. After she had gone, he said, mainly to himself, "All I ever wanted was to be a good writer."

When the plane was finally called, I kissed the three men goodbye, feeling genuine affection for each. But with David the electricity was still present, so much so that I felt we must be covered by St. Elmo's fire. Afterward, I was in a state of pleasant shock. I didn't feel guilty, since I hadn't done anything to betray Daniel. What I had felt had been unbidden, beyond my control. Although I was not blind to the possibility, I didn't think there was a real chance that this lightning would strike twice.

In fact, Daniel was dearer to me then more than ever. He was my hero, and not mine alone. In CORE, he was developing a reputation as a strategist and spokesman, and as a personal risk taker. He read Carl von Clausewitz as well as Saul Alinsky and Gandhi to become a more effective opponent of racial discrimination. Not only had he mobilized the Newspaper Guild's participation in the march, he had negotiated a pension plan at the publishing company where he worked. This had required him to get members of the company's guild, which was stuffed with prima-donna writers and editors who were experts in labor-relations law, to authorize a strike. After the vote to strike, he had been locked in acrimonious negotiations for two days and nights at the Federal Mediation and Conciliation Service. After the company capitulated, everybody was suddenly angry with him because the international guild had not authorized the local guild to strike in the first place. Daniel had believed it when he'd told coworkers that the international guild would support a strike, but a local official who wanted to compete for an international office had lied to him. He called a meeting of all the parties involved, but didn't attend it himself.

A few months later, Daniel received an award as Washington's Guildsman of the Year for successfully representing his bargaining unit and for organizing the guild's participation in the March on Washington. He wanted to blow most of the prize money on a trip to New York to see Baldwin's play *Blues for Mister Charlie,* so I called James from the hotel where the award had been presented, and told him we would go to New York tomorrow to see his play if it was still possible to get tickets. This would be the last preview performance before opening night and was completely sold out, Jimmy said.

"But don't worry, baby, I'll get you in."

He asked if we had a place to stay and I suddenly felt as if my knees might buckle. What if he offered to have David put us up? I told him I thought we had that covered but would get back to him if it didn't work out.

"Fine, baby!"

We arranged to get together the next afternoon at the Russian Tearoom; and I next called our friend Isabelle on Minetta Lane, who was torn between her desire to see us and her aversion to cleaning her apartment. It wasn't that she liked living with the New York soot that filtered through screens and even closed windows, but she hated disturbing anything in her small apartment after she had found the perfect place to put it. After I said that we wouldn't stay if she dusted, Isabelle insisted that we stay with her.

Knowing my aversion to dirt, Daniel wondered why I had rejected Jimmy's offer to arrange a place for us to stay. Although he didn't pursue the subject further, I don't think he was completely satisfied by my answer, "I think we shouldn't abandon old friends just because we've made new ones. Besides, you love the Village and we have lots of friends there we want to see." All of that was true, but it was also true that I didn't know for certain how I would react when I was with David.

Jack O'Dell was with James when we joined them at the Russian Tearoom. By then I had read Jack's essay in *Freedomways* about corporate power in the South and I considered it a brilliant illumination of the hidden pillars of apartheid. I told him so, but obviously Jack had stepped on powerful toes. As James had predicted, J. Edgar Hoover hammered Jack, using as his anvil a compliant journalist published in over two hundred newspapers. Three days before we got together at New York's swankiest tearoom, nationally syndicated columnist Joseph Alsop published an article alleging Communist Party infiltration of the civil rights movement and citing Jack as the prime nefarious example. Alsop said Martin Luther King, Jr., had dropped O'Dell after being advised by government officials that Jack was "the genuine Communist article." Alsop also wrote that King had originally been dedicated to nonviolence, "Yet he has accepted and is almost certainly still accepting Communist collaboration and even Communist advice." In passing, Alsop smeared a devoutly Christian and nonviolent civil rights leader, SNCC's John Lewis. Referring to SNCC as "Snick", Alsop said that, although not a red, Lewis "quite frankly believes in quasi-insurrectionary tactics. Thus no great difference has been made in Snick's tactics, because known Communists have also begun to play a certain role in Snick."

"That hatchet job had Big Brother's fingerprints all over it," Baldwin observed.

"He also said there are communists in CORE," Daniel noted, "but he didn't name names, because he thinks King is 'the prime communist target.'"

I didn't know what Jack's political affiliations were, but I was keenly aware that my father had once considered himself a communist and was now risking his skin to smuggle people out of East Germany. Both he and I were opposed to the USSR's undemocratic structure and its oppressive domestic and foreign policies, but we practiced many of the professed ideals it had betrayed. I knew though that Jack's consuming purpose was to combat racism, as my father's aim had been to fight fascism. Jack's attackers surely knew that he had worked for King as a "direct-mail fundraiser," using innovative computer technology and threatening nothing American except apartheid. He was a technician, not a policymaker, but as a private citizen he had offended powerful capitalists and southern politicians, and the FBI had painted him red and used him to discredit King and nonviolent rights groups that engaged in civil disobedience. I told Jack that I hoped he would sue for slander. He said he was seriously considering doing that.

We went from the Russian Tearoom to the theater, where stagehands were working on the set and actors were talking and rehearsing bits of action. To illustrate his view of the play's message, someone told a story, which he attributed to Lightnin' Hopkins, about a small boy who had tried to tell the owner of a cotton rolling mill that it was on fire. The boy had stood before the mill owner, breathless and too excited to get the words out. Listening to him stammer, the man finally told the boy to sing if he couldn't speak. So the boy had sung out, "Oooooooh saaaay, Mr. Charlie, your rooooooolling mill is burrrrrning down!"

I could see David, who had a role in his brother's play, rehearsing on the other side of the stage, and I could tell that he had seen me, but he didn't come over for several minutes. When he came, he looked stunned and I again felt covered by St. Elmo's fire. Hours later, after the play, we were able to talk normally because, like everyone else in the theater, we were emotionally drained. Whatever the long-term merits of the drama, the cast apparently believed that it was as immediately important as an approaching fire. Rip Torn was so caught up in his role as the violent white landowner who was in love with his black victim's wife that he couldn't party afterward with the Baldwins and a few of their friends. David also was upset, but for a different reason. He said he had never performed so poorly before, fluffing lines and fumbling a prop, and he attributed it to my presence in the audience. At his request, I promised not to attend opening night.

To get to the party, we split into two groups so that I could hail a cab for one foursome and Daniel could do the same for the other, since New York cab drivers were notoriously reluctant to stop for black fares. Although neither Daniel nor I knew it at the time, the party was a birthday celebration for an actor who was the younger brother of a woman we both loved and admired in Washington. Beautiful Bernice Hooks lived in a housing project in Anacostia, DC's most dangerously neglected section, where she organized plays, basketball teams, and other athletic and educational events for the young people, enlisting her friends' frequent participation. She always had one or two and sometimes three children living with her in addition to her own; and she imparted, to every child in the project, the knowledge that they had friends who cared about them. Her brother had become interested in theater by acting in her ghetto productions, and she had kept us informed of Bobby Dean's progress after he left DC for New York.

When I arrived at the party, the guest of honor introduced himself as Robert Hooks and was startled, but happily so, when I called him Bobby Dean and kissed and hugged him warmly. David was also taken aback, but Daniel, having arrived first, had made the connection earlier and had kept quiet so as not to spoil my surprise. Together we explained that we not only knew and cherished Bernice, but were also friends of his older brother, Charley, and had partied with his older sister and a younger brother. We attended family reunions, so meeting Bobby Dean, or Robert Hooks, was like encountering a relative I had heard a lot about but never before met. After we brought him up to date on family doings in DC, he told us that he was currently performing in a play called *Dutchman* by a young black playwright named LeRoi Jones. He said he would very much like for us to see the play, which was at the Cherry Lane Theatre, a short walk from Isabelle's apartment, and tell him our reactions afterward.

The party reminded me of a steamy scene in Baldwin's novel *Another Country*, in which the two protagonists got carried away and made love in a dark alcove in an apartment where others were reveling. I wasn't certain, but I thought that the character in the book had also been the only white woman present. Bobby Dean Hooks' birthday party comprised mainly actors, comedians, musicians, designers, writers, and other artists or entertainers, and seemed much more convivial than the fictional gathering. Humorous anecdotes and witticisms, almost always self-deprecating or ironically aggrandizing, were swiftly followed by raucous laughter augmented by mannered hand and body movements. At one point, I wandered into a dimly lit bedroom and discovered Jimmy Baldwin alone and looking rather forlorn. It seemed incredible that the most outspoken man in America could look so lost. As we talked quietly, someone I hadn't met came up and handed him a hand-rolled cigarette, then pulled out a silver-plated Zippo and lit it for him. Jimmy took a couple of puffs, reminding me again of Crawford, and then handed it to me. I had smelled but never smoked marijuana before, and I did my best to keep my cool as I inhaled more deeply than when I smoked mere tobacco. I coughed, however, and rather violently. So of course I took several more drags to demonstrate that I could handle it.

The rest of the evening was not only highly enjoyable—I was able to converse attentively, dance, and fully experience music, simultaneously—it was also a period of remarkable emotional clarity. I was still attracted to David, and after sharing another reefer I was so randy that I began to look around for a dark alcove. But it was Daniel with whom I wanted to make love.

The next day we went to see *Dutchman* and afterward had drinks with Bobby Dean. He had performed as well as his part allowed and then some. But the play obviously had been written around the strikingly original role of the white femme fatale. As startling as a switchblade, in one act Jones, who later changed his "slave" name to Amiri Baraka, said as much about race relations up north as Baldwin's magnum opus conveyed about oppression down south. Both plays dealt with interracial sex and the murder of a young black man by a white person, but Jones shocked and surprised audiences with his fresh insights into pathological racism, while Baldwin's play raged against an all-too-familiar American tragedy.

Blues for Mister Charlie was dedicated to the memory of Medgar Evers and the children who had been killed in the Birmingham church bombing. On the first day of the summer of 1964, while audiences were watching *Blues* at the Actors Studio Theatre in New York, yet another national tragedy was unfolding in Neshoba County, Mississippi. Three civil rights workers, James Chaney, Michael Schwerner, and Andrew Goodman, who were investigating a church bombing in the county, had suddenly disappeared. The three activists were part of the rights movement's plan to enlist roughly a thousand middle-class college students, most of whom were white, in the struggle for voting rights. The idea was to have students from outside the South live in Mississippi's black communities for the summer, to teach, serve, learn from, and help organize the Mississippi Freedom Democratic Party. After the summer, the students were expected to return to their own communities and universities and tell their experiences. The fruit of what was to become known as "Freedom Summer" would be an integrated challenge to Mississippi's whites-only delegation to the Democratic Party's National Convention in late August.

Because all three of the missing activists were CORE members, the national organization sent Lou Smith, a good friend and one of national CORE's most courageous troubleshooters, to investigate. The young men were still missing when Lou returned to New York days later, stopping in DC to talk with people in the Justice Department and coming by our house to catch his breath. He told us that there was virtually no chance that Chaney, Schwerner, and Goodman were still alive. They had gone to Neshoba County a day or so before the arrival of the students, to investigate the church bombing and the beating of three local African Americans but had been promptly arrested and taken to jail in the nearby town of Philadelphia, Mississippi. The local sheriff said they had been released around ten o'clock that night and that he had no idea what had happened to them since. In Lou's opinion, the young men had been murdered by the Klan with the help of police and possibly other officials. He said the standard response of state and local officials and most of the local press was that there was nothing to investigate, that the three had probably "chickened out" and gone home, or were hiding somewhere, possibly Cuba, hoping to tarnish the reputation of "the great state of Mississippi." John Doar, Thelton's old boss at Justice, had been seriously concerned from day one, Lou added, but the FBI in Mississippi had at first turned its back, saying it didn't think any federal law was broken. He said local CORE and SNCC should step up the pressure on the Justice Department to investigate, just in case the young men were still alive and being held somewhere.

This was the beginning of what would frequently be referred to in the media as a "long hot summer," a tag borrowed from William Faulkner, who had lived and worked among the rednecks who were the source of most of his heat. DC CORE picketed the Justice Department, and when there was no apparent progress in discovering what had become of our missing comrades, we and SNCC mounted a candlelight vigil at the building's entrance. During that period, I practically lived in the SNCC's Washington office, constantly on the phone arranging for three people with burning candles to be in front of Justice's door for four three-hour shifts every day.

When the bodies of the three martyrs were finally found, brutally murdered and buried under an earthen dam in Neshoba County, it was time to prepare for demonstrations at the Democratic National Convention to support the seating of Mississippi's Freedom Democrats, instead of the state's traditional whites-only delegation. To avoid the appearance of picking on Democrats, this meant that massive demonstrations also had to be mounted for the earlier Republican National Convention at the Cow Palace in San Francisco. Since the Democratic Convention would be in Atlantic

City, SNCC and CORE were calling on groups in eastern cities to send busloads of people to sit, stand, and sleep on the famous boardwalk, gavel to gavel.

The problem for DC CORE was that most of its members were government employees—I said we were bourgeois—and forbidden by the Hatch Act from participating in certain political activities. Aware of every devilish detail in his town, LBJ announced that such shenanigans at his nominating convention were definitely "Hatched" and would be fiercely prosecuted. By that time, DC CORE Chairman Julius Hobson had been deposed for undemocratic conduct, and the new chairman announced that he would not organize a demonstration that might cost most members their livelihoods as well as their liberty. He added that he was resigning as chairman since he had resigned his government job to teach at Wayne State University in Detroit. In the confusion that followed, I was drafted into organizing those who weren't subject to the Hatch Act or would defy the ban. And soon, I and a lovable wild man from Bronx CORE named Herb Calendar tried to recruit students at Howard University to participate in the Atlantic City demonstration. It was depressing to see how many young people at the university would leave the job of defeating discrimination to a tiny handful of fellow students, but when the opening gavel banged in Atlantic City, there were two busloads from DC on—and sometimes under—the boardwalk.

Chapter Seven

Going to Mississippi 1964

Already president of the United States in August of 1964, Lyndon B. Johnson was the unseen helmsman who kept the Democratic National Convention in Atlantic City moving on course toward his nomination, despite southerly headwinds pushing for changes. He had prepared for the challenge of Mississippi's Freedom Democrats, who demanded that an integrated delegation represent the state, by seeing to it that level-headed leaders of the civil rights movement, including Martin Luther King, Jr., Roy Wilkins, Whitney Young, and Bayard Rustin, received VIP treatment and remained firmly in his corner. He had even arranged at the last minute to have an African American woman, Patricia Harris, second his nomination. But the master political strategist was not about to unseat the "regular" all-white delegation from Mississippi, since he believed this would trigger not one, but several, walkouts by southern delegations, creating a schism that almost certainly would cost him the election. He was, as we would come to realize, almost as insecure as he was masterful.

What LBJ hadn't counted on was that a dark star within the Freedom delegation would testify at the convention and begin to shine on millions of television screens until her down-home brilliance would briefly eclipse his own. Despite frantic countermeasures to curtail her time on TV, Fannie Lou Hamer's personal magnetism lifted the convention hall off its moorings and almost carried it out to sea. She was a sharecropper's daughter and a courageous activist who had not been silenced by a near-fatal jailhouse beating. Television viewers could see that suffering in her glazed eyes and hear it in her hoarse voice as she told what rule by white supremacists was doing to black Mississippians.

While debate fumed inside the convention hall, protesters on the nearby boardwalk sat and socialized and listened to rumors of impending direct action. We also listened to pep talks by such CORE or SNCC stalwarts as David Dennis, Stokely Carmichael, and my friend from the march, Ed Brown. Three weeks earlier, Dennis had delivered the eulogy for James Chaney, one of the three CORE members slain in Neshoba County. Here as there, Dennis talked passionately about the failure of government officials to protect the lives of rights workers and blacks who wanted to vote. Ed was sometimes didactic, other times ironic, suggesting that President Johnson needed the black vote to carry Mississippi. Stokely liked to shock—possibly a trait he picked up in a mostly-Jewish, Bronx high school—saying things like, "The first man to give his life for the American Revolution was a black man, Crispus Attucks. Crispus Attucks was a fool!" He also argued that Goldwater conservatives talked tough, but liberals were more likely to drop the bomb. He was serious, however, in his sometimes off-key attempts to instill black pride. I think he was envious of a group of Young Democrats who violently broke up a counterdemonstration to ours by the American Nazi Party.

Everyone on the boardwalk was delighted to learn that, apparently in response to Fannie Lou Hamer's testimony, the convention had offered to seat some Freedom Democrats. And most of us were proud when they turned the offer down despite being advised by every national rights leader and even their own attorney to accept. The offer was for two seats as nonvoting, at-large delegates, separated from Mississippi's all-white delegation. Insisting as a matter of principle that they would only accept seats with voting rights inside the recognized delegation took courage, since the state and some local governments had threatened to prosecute Freedom Democrats for trying to unseat "official delegates," and the deal would have been helpful in their defense. At one point, demonstrators made a rather half-hearted attempt at a "sit in" in the convention hall. We rather soon backed off, but some Freedom Democrats took delegates' seats in the Mississippi section and refused to leave. Whether that was the only reason or not, the all-white delegation walked out and denounced the convention.

The white press depicted the Freedom Democrats' rejection of "the compromise" as worse than wrong-headed—more like simple-minded subversion—and several people, blacks as well as whites, came to the boardwalk to scold us. One of the scolds was the woman who had been recruited at the last minute to second the nomination (and who later would become the first black woman to have a Cabinet seat). She gave Daniel such a dressing down that he remained depressed until Bayard Rustin came out and, with an assist by Ed Brown, climbed onto the table that served as our speaker's platform. As camera crews rushed over, he launched into a long recital of all the hardships he had experienced in the movement—the beatings, the jail time, the slanderous attacks—how weary he was after years of hard, frustrating work, with little to show for it but scars.

"Now," he said, "the only thing that keeps me going, the only thing that gives me the strength to get up in the morning, get dressed, and get back to work,"—here he paused to scan the open-mouthed audience—"is gin!" As we erupted into applause, he raised a bottle he had been holding half-hidden by a pant-leg and took a big swig. He went on to say that the Freedom delegation had been absolutely right to reject the window-dressing offer, "because now the Democrats are forced to make real reforms that will end racial exclusion within the party." He ended by urging us to return to our communities to organize voting blocs, and then work "vigilantly" to make the politicians we elect "less dishonest."

Ed was smiling broadly as he helped his former mentor down from the table, but I think he was also misty-eyed. A couple of years earlier, Rustin had given Ed a watercolor painting that he had acquired while in India absorbing the teachings of Gandhi. After the March on Washington, Ed had given the painting to me for helping him translate writing by Karl Marx from its original German text. I doubted that the painting actually came from Gandhi—that would have been too much—but I had no doubt that super-macho Ed, who liked to wear a black beret, black turtleneck, and shades, really loved the old rogue.

On the last night of the convention, Daniel had already departed for DC and I was sitting on the boardwalk with more than a hundred other demonstrators, all of us bone tired and homesick for clean sheets, when I was suddenly overcome by the celebration of LBJ's birthday. I must have known vaguely that celebrants would be releasing balloons or something to mark the occasion, but I was completely unprepared for the sight and sound of fireworks exploding directly overhead. Literally in a flash, it felt like 1943 instead of 1964, and I felt like I was again in Hamburg, Germany, at the center of a firestorm created by an armada of British bombers. Completely terrified, I must have curled up in a fetal position and begun to wail and cry. Soon, however, I came back to the moment, and became aware of the soothing words being spoken to me, the hands stroking me, and the bodies shielding me from danger. After hearing me babble about bombs and burning bodies, someone told me that we were only experiencing harmless fireworks. I think I

By Norman Driscoll, Staff Photographer

Mom's on Picket Duty

Daniel Ingram, 3½, waits beside the White House fence while his mother does duty in yesterday's picket line made up of civil rights demonstrators.

A *Washington Post* article featuring a photograph of my son, Daniel, in line with me during a rights demonstration in Washington, DC.

An Appeal to You from

JAMES FARMER
Congress of Racial Equality

JOHN LEWIS
Student Non-violent Coordinating Committee

ROY WILKINS
National Association for the Advancement of Colored People

MARTIN LUTHER KING, JR.
Southern Christian Leadership Conference

A. PHILIP RANDOLPH
Negro American Labor Council

WHITNEY YOUNG
National Urban League

to MARCH on WASHINGTON

WEDNESDAY AUGUST 28, 1963

America faces a crisis . . .
Millions of Negroes are denied freedom . . .
Millions of citizens, black and white, are unemployed . . .

We demand:
— Meaningful Civil Rights Laws
— Massive Federal Works Program
— Full and Fair Employment
— Decent Housing
— The Right to Vote
— Adequate Integrated Education

In our community, groups and individuals are mobilizing for the August 28th demonstration. For information regarding your participation, call the local Coordinating Committee for the

MARCH ON WASHINGTON FOR JOBS AND FREEDOM

1417 You Street, N.W. ADams 2-2320

CO-CHAIRMEN

Rev. Walter E. Fauntroy, Coordinator
Joseph A. Beavers
E. Charles Brown

Edward A. Hailes
Julius W. Hobson
Sterling Tucker

A flyer for the March on Washington, where Martin Luther King, Jr. gave his iconic "I have a dream" speech.

200 Guildsmen Join March On Washington

Locals Hoist ANG Banner For Equality

More than 200 Guildsmen joined 200,000 other civil-rights advocates who marched on Washington Aug. 28 in the largest demonstration ever witnessed in the nation's capital.

They were among more than 50,000 members of 31 unions who turned out to demonstrate support for ending discrimination in every aspect of the nation's life.

The largest Guild contingent marched under the New York Local banner. Eighty-two members led by Joseph Eisenberg and Frank Irwin of the New York Times Unit and Leonard Weeks of Consumer Reports came in two buses of a 50-bus UAW caravan.

A carload of North Jersey Guildsmen headed by Barbara Finkelstein, local secretary, joined the marchers from ANG headquarters behind a big ANG banner carried by Secretary-Treasurer

Additional Civil Rights Story, Pictures . . . Page 5

Charles A. Perlik and Research and Information Director Ellis T. Baker, who is in charge of the Guild's human-rights program.

Alabama Strike Achieves Pay Increases Up To $36

Daniel leads the way for the newspaper guild.

A flyer for the March on Washington. "We Shall Overcome" was a popular protest song.

Mississippi

America's Number 1 Police State

— HEAR —

MRS. FANNIE LOU HAMER

First Negro Women to Run for Congress from the State of Mississippi.

SPEAK ON:

"THE MISSISSIPPI FREEDOM DEMOCRATIC PARTY and THE LONG HOT SUMMER"

ALSO HEAR

Mrs. ELLA BAKER

Rev. WALTER FAUNTROY

Rev. CHARLES SHERROD,

Albany, Georgia

Tues: July 21st., 1964 — 8:00 p. m

New Bethel Baptist Church

812 S St. N W.

An advertisement for a speech by Fannie Lou Hamer, an acclaimed rights activist and the first African American woman from Mississippi to run for Congress.

By Wally McNamee, Staff Photographer

NEW CITIZEN MARIONE INGRAM
. . . a survivor of persecution now fights it here

Death Camp Survivor Joins Rights Drive

Marione Ingram heard the the fireworks exploding at the Democratic National Convention last week and had difficulty convincing herself that she was not hearing the bombs she narrowly escaped in her native Germany during World War II.

"I was absolutely terrified," she said yesterday. "Of course I knew better, but I could hardly believe it wasn't really the bombs."

It is because of those wartime memories that she has become active in the civil rights struggle here. "I just can't get over the feeling that as long as anyone is being persecuted, it can happen to me again," she said.

Mrs. Ingram, who is 27 and the mother of a 3-year-old son, became a U.S. citizen two days ago. She became interested in the civil rights movement when she worked as a volunteer in the March on Washington a year ago.

She said that although things in this country are far from perfect, she is grateful that here at least she is permitted to protest what she calls "oppressive conditions" for Negroes.

A *Washington Post* article on how the fireworks at the Democratic National Convention, in Mississippi, reminded me of the bombs I heard in Germany during World War II.

Neil Chassman
The Fieldson School
Fieldston Rd.
Riverdale, Bronx 71, NY

October 10, 1964

Dear Neil Chassman,

Ellen Maslow referred your letter to me, and I am delighted that you want to adopt a Freedom School. The process of adoption is a matter of money, books, and a lot of correspondence in terms of letters, poems, stories, paintings, etc.--real communication.

Enclosed is the list of books which we need immediately. Whatever you can send. And the money thing can be arranged with the specific school you work with. May I suggest perhaps Pascagoula, which is on the Gulf Coast, where the coordinator is a woman from New York and Washington, D.C., a Mrs. Marione Ingram. She is French, and is doing fantastic things with the kids, both children and teen-agers. The address is 604 du Pont. You may take it over from there, and ask her what she needs.

Enclosed also is a statement about what the Freedom Schools mean in terms of the complexity of Mississippi, and a now out-of-state summary of activity in the Freedom Schools-Community-Centers all over the state. You will notice that Pascagoula had not yet started yet; you can be in on the beginning. Marione will welcome your concern, and I'm sure some kind of exchange can be arranged, both for kids and teachers, especially for vacations.

Take it--

Yours for freedom,

Liz Fusco, Coordinator
COFO Freedom Schools

Enclosure

cc: Marione Ingram

A letter from Liz Fusco, coordinator of the freedom schools, about a donation of school supplies she suggested be made to my freedom school.

THE VOICE OF THE MOVEMENT

The Freedom Voice of the Fifth Congressional District (COFO)

609 Bowen Street, Moss Point, Mississippi 475-7055

Hi baby:
Hope all is well with you = I am doing well.
Sending along a letter, which says something nice about me.
Is your cold better?
Please take care. 'cause I love you - Ahh-
Weather is miserable today.
I miss you and that little monster-
Say hey to everyone for me-
the #1 word in Miss is
'MOTHER-FUCKING' this
and Mother-fucking that.
and you told me to watch my language-

Please write =

All my love —

Freedom

Marione

ONE MAN - ONE JOB
ONE MAN - ONE VOTE

A letter I wrote to Daniel while in Mississippi. I let him know that I had begun cursing, even though he'd advised me to watch my language.

When I returned to Moss Point in 2013, the city and its people were much different than I remembered them. Among other things, a new city hall replaced the old one, which had been destroyed in 2005 by Hurricane Katrina.

On my return to Moss Point, I was moved to be able to talk with former students of my freedom school, including Aneice Liddell (far left, next to me) who became the first African American to be elected mayor of Moss Point.

Me in front of Burnham Drugs, where I and a group of African American friends were refused service after the Freedom Vote in 1964. We were told, "We don't serve Niggers!", and when my companion refuted, "We didn't ask for Niggers. We want banana splits!" we were kicked out of the restaurant and I was arrested.

I told our experience to a black waitress in Burnham Drugs and she was shocked and appalled.

understood fairly quickly, but it took a while to recover enough to fall asleep with my head in a warm lap.

The next day, I was fine and glad to be folding my invisible tent, trading addresses with new friends, and checking bus passenger lists. I was looking forward to going home to Daniel and my son, and, while I hadn't thought much about it during the past month, the following morning was scheduled to be an exceedingly important one for me. If I made it to a certain federal court in Baltimore by 9 a.m., I would be sworn in as a citizen of the United States. It had taken quite a long time to reach this brink. Probably because of my association with civil rights groups, I had been made to undergo a more extensive investigation than others and to produce two people who could vouch for me during every six-month period since I had arrived in 1952. For some reason that was never explained, no one could vouch for me for more than a six-month stretch, but my friends had apparently come through and I was scheduled to be sworn in. Events and duties on our last day in Atlantic City took longer than expected, however, and it was after dark when I realized that I had sent off the last DC bus with an empty seat—the one I should have been seated in! No worry, I'd hitch a ride, I thought. But all of the sudden, there was no one left who was going my way. I began to feel ridiculous and somewhat desperate, since I doubted that the court would give me a second chance at citizenship anytime soon. Someone suggested that I try to get on the Freedom Democrats' bus, which was late in departing and would pass by Washington on its way south. I raced across the parking lot to the bus and breathlessly threw myself at the mercy of a beautiful young woman with a clipboard who was standing outside the open door. She interrupted my explanation with a terse:

"Sorry, there are no empty seats."

While I caught my breath and considered what to do next, a hoarse voice within the bus called out:

"Child, you take my seat; I'll find something."

Before I or the young woman with the clipboard could respond, two warm hands pulled me up into the bus and held me until I and the young woman accepted the fact that Fannie Lou Hamer was going to share her seat with me.

Although it was after midnight before the bus departed, neither of us slept that night. Instead, we told each other stories about where we had come from and how and why we had landed in Atlantic City. Our journeys had been so wildly different. It seemed incredible but at the same time inevitable that we would be sitting together. In the darkness, I felt like we were traveling through space rather than down a highway. Ms. Hamer may also have felt that our encounter was special, because she made certain that this was only the beginning of our relationship.

Except for Daniel, I almost never talked with anyone, especially someone I just met, about painful childhood experiences such as the one I had relived the night before. Out of character, I'd let a *Washington Post* reporter who had heard about it interview me earlier in the day, and he'd asked a number of questions about disturbing events. Perhaps because those freshly aroused memories were still with me and I still felt sheepish about the episode, and because I was with a strong woman who had experienced violent racial hatred, I opened up about how I had felt as a child, and how I felt then, as an adult. She tactfully let me know that she had heard about the incident on the boardwalk, but that she didn't know the details of it. She didn't register any surprise when I told her that, as Jews, my mother and I had been denied entry to a bomb shelter and even a church during air raids. Only later did she say that she had guessed when I entered the bus that I might be the one who had been upset by the fireworks. Because she looked and spoke like my idea of a wise Sybil of ancient lore, I didn't ask how she had figured that out.

Ms. Hamer's eyes were sad and her tone was serious, but she smiled and laughed as we talked. She laughed both softly and at times raucously. She laughed at the Klan and the Citizens Councils, at the self-righteousness of politicians, at the bafflement of friends, at the cruelty of the police, at the naiveté of northern college boys, and at screw-ups in the movement. The beating that pulped her flesh had not weakened her will or her sense of humor. She made Mississippi sound like some not-to-be-missed, hell-on-wheels attraction. Compelled to work in the fields from childhood on and treated like dirt by whites, she nevertheless loved her state, and not just the black people in it. She didn't say this, but it was evident in her determination to fight there until she or Jim Crow was dead. From time to time, when the laughter subsided, she'd squeeze my hand and her face would turn solemn. "Child, you got to promise to come. It's more important now that the college boys have gone back home. They helped us get started, but we got to keep on going, or . . ." She shook her head and looked out the window at the night shadows racing past.

I told her about Daniel and Danny and her smile returned as broad as ever.

"Bring your boy and your man, too!" she said. "This is all about the children. White folks there ain't never going to accept me, but we've got to make room for the children. We've got to give them a chance, and I know you can help."

Her words and mine reverberated in my body as I promised to go to Mississippi. I think my body knew that I had been on the way for a long time.

I was not at all tired when I stepped from the bus onto the outskirts of Washington, still warmed by Fannie Lou Hamer's parting embrace. The slanting sunlight was welcome, however, since I was the only person at that wide spot in the road, and I was elated when my husband, whom I had called at four a.m. from a rest stop, arrived not long after the bus pulled away. With Daniel was Laura, a friend, who was holding our son who was holding a tiny American flag in each fist, Laura's gesture to celebrate my imminent citizenship.

Laura's skin was the same color as Ms. Hamer's, but was smooth and creamy, never having been seen by the Mississippi sun, and was set off by a white silk blouse cut rather low. My son had on his black cowboy hat and a denim jacket covered with civil-rights buttons. With my husband, who was wearing a dark blazer, they made me aware of my disheveled appearance: jeans and a man's shirt in which I had slept on the boardwalk for three nights, unbrushed hair hanging down my back, and a somewhat battered button on my breast that advocated "one man one vote." But there was no time to freshen up. Laura took the wheel, I took Danny, and my husband took a city bus to his office in DC. Although we arrived late, it was another forty-five minutes before someone shouted "all rise!" and the judge finally made his entrance.

Wearing his black robe and sitting behind a desk much higher than the assembled aspirants, the judge tried to impress upon us how fortunate we were to be obtaining American citizenship. He told us that this is the land of opportunity, where anyone can climb as high as his abilities will take him. He also said there were forty-eight of us and that we came from forty-eight different countries, which provoked a murmur and caused many to look discreetly at the people around them. Laura and I craned our necks, but she was the only person of African descent to be seen. Most of the people looked like affluent Europeans, and I began to feel let down, but Laura flashed me a brilliant smile that seemed to say, "Don't let anything discourage you."

Fortunately, the judge's sermon was brief. He ignored the civil rights struggle and the escalating war in Vietnam and talked in solemn tones about "shouldering the responsibilities of citizenship," which I took to be a reference to the fact that every applicant, regardless of age, sex, or physical condition, had been required to affirm that he or she would be willing to bear arms on America's behalf. When he finished, an oath of allegiance was administered en masse, with Laura and Danny joining in delightedly. This was followed by the formal handing out of individual certificates of citizenship, each one rolled up and tied with a red ribbon.

A "lady" from the Daughters of the American Revolution (DAR), the judge said, would hand out the certificates. The "lady," a woman in her fifties wearing a pink and white striped cotton suit and a pink blouse with a frilly collar that peeked over the rim of her jacket, took a position beside the clerk, in front of the judge's desk, and smiled broadly without parting audaciously crimson lips. A pink pillbox hat of the type made popular by Jackie Kennedy topped golden parlor curls. White gloves and shoes completed her outfit.

As our names were called in alphabetical order, each new citizen walked up to the DAR lady to receive a certificate, which she daintily held aloft in her gloved left hand. Before handing it over she would say "Welcome to America," and then she'd bestow her broad smile and offer a white-cotton-glove handshake along with the simulated parchment. When it came my turn, Laura walked beside me carrying Danny. But the sight of the three of us apparently curdled whatever coursed through blue DAR veins. The woman's eyes glazed in horror as if we were vermin approaching to rip off her pink clothes and leave her exposed before all these foreigners. Both her hands retreated and her gaping crimson mouth turned down until it resembled the mask of tragedy. Not certain what to do, I curtsied, smiled, and extended my right hand. After it became clear that she could not bring herself to give me the certificate, which she held slightly behind her derrière, I stepped forward and snatched it from her gloved hand.

"Fuck you, lady." I said it pleasantly, but loud enough for those nearby to hear. Then I curtsied again, and Laura, Danny, and I turned and walked up the aisle toward the courtroom door. Before we reached it, Danny started waving his flags and singing, "We Shall Overcome." Struggling to control our laughter, Laura and I chimed in.

In the week that followed, I made preparations for an extended sojourn in Mississippi. As Fannie Lou Hamer had suggested, I volunteered to work for the Student Nonviolent Coordinating Committee and was given instruction in nonviolent direct action by SNCC students at Howard University. I also received numerous warnings from friends inside and outside "the movement." The murderers of Chaney, Schwerner, and Goodman were still free, Lou Smith reminded me, "with their rifles racked in their pickup trucks and their white hoods in their back pockets." Both he and the instructors insisted that the two months before the election would be exceptionally dangerous ones for rights workers. Our primary job would be to register African American voters and get them to the poll—capital offenses in Mississippi. Neither Lou nor any of the instructors told me not to go, but Lou worried out loud about security, and the instructors tried hard during the training to provoke me, to see if I would "blow my cool."

The instructors' attitudes toward nonviolence were diverse. A few embraced it out of personal convictions; others saw it as a necessary tactic, but questioned whether it could succeed in our violent society. All, however, were willing to surrender their right to self-defense to achieve their goal, which was to raise an entire people from a condition akin to serfdom.

Daniel never suggested that I not go to Mississippi, even though, having grown up in the South, he was painfully aware of the dangers. He joked that I wouldn't last long because I couldn't stomach his mother's southern cooking. However, he readily admitted that she wasn't much of a cook. But when my mother asked him on the phone to forbid me to go, Daniel told her that she should know better than anybody that telling her daughter not to go wouldn't work.

"I would break both my legs if I thought that would stop her," he added, "but she feels she has to go because of what happened in Germany."

Mother didn't respond, but immediately hung up the telephone, causing Daniel to feel terribly guilty. He wanted to call her back and apologize, but I told him she wouldn't discuss the past, even with me. It was still too painful for her. Nevertheless, I hoped that my going to Mississippi might somehow bring us closer. My father had responded to my decision with great warmth. Like Daniel, he understood that I had to go. Like my mother, several members of DC CORE told me I shouldn't "abandon" my child. In answer, I echoed Fannie Lou Hamer; I told them I was doing it for the children, theirs and mine as well as those in Mississippi.

While SNCC considered my application and debated the role of whites in the struggle for black freedom, I bought a bus ticket for Jackson, Mississippi, having decided that I would go, regardless, and that a bus would be the least conspicuous way. I had promised Fannie Lou Hamer that I would come and I knew that she would find useful work for me to do once I got there. As it turned out, my acceptance by SNCC as a "field worker" came through before the departure date. I was told to report to SNCC headquarters on Lynch Street in Jackson, where I would be briefed on my assignment to a team working out of the town of Moss Point. At the Trailways bus terminal in Washington, DC, I promised my husband that I would be very careful. I promised Danny that I would bring him a red fire engine. And I got Laura, who thought Stokely Carmichael was one of the planet's sexiest men, to dry her eyes and laugh, by promising to bring her the earring he sometimes wore.

Lou Smith had suggested I take Trailways because he thought the Klan wouldn't expect me to be on it, since that bus company was being boycotted by CORE to protest its lack of black drivers and clerks. Lou didn't like what he called "the security situation" in the COFO district in which I would be working, which was next to the one in which the three rights workers had been murdered. COFO stood for Council of Federated Organizations, the umbrella group for civil rights organizations that participated in Freedom Summer. At summer's end, most of those organizations pulled out of Mississippi or severely reduced staff there, leaving mainly SNCC, a few CORE workers, and local NAACP chapters to maximize black participation in November's state-wide elections, both the official balloting and the parallel Freedom Vote that welcomed rather than rejected African Americans. According to Lou Smith, the absence of other mainstream civil rights and religious organizations made security for SNCC workers little more than a shadow. "So stay in touch and don't be afraid to pull up stakes and run," he warned.

It was still summer and the bus ride was long and hot. There wasn't much to do on it but read, look out the window, and think about Danny and Daniel or about Lou Smith's instruction that I not be afraid to run. The closer we came to Mississippi, the redder the earth became and the worse the houses looked. Many were dilapidated shacks sitting on small piles of rocks, but still inhabited. I became apprehensive when two men with lined red necks took an interest in me at some awful-smelling rest stop. Seeing a bunch of soldiers milling about, I took refuge in their midst, asking if one of them could give me a match and receiving several packets plus a lighter in return. The suspect rednecks immediately lost all interest, which was a welcome relief although I couldn't keep my hands from shaking slightly as I lit up.

Stokely Carmichael wasn't at SNCC headquarters in Jackson, so I didn't get to see whether he actually wore an earring, but the beautiful young woman who had been standing outside the Freedom Democrats' bus in Atlantic City was there. She told me the name of the project leader in Moss Point and said that in addition to working in the voter registration drive, I would be expected to start a Freedom School in Pascagoula, a larger city on the Gulf Cost. I would also help the black shipyard workers in Pascagoula get organized. When I mentioned that I had never taught school before, she smiled and said that I was obviously a fast learner. She gave me the name of a woman I could call for advice and some supplies, but made it clear that I would have to improvise and make do.

Courtland Cox, a largish man with a New York accent who exuded warmth, gave me further instruction on nonviolence and the dangers we faced. Like Stokely Carmichael, he had gone to Howard University and been active in DC civil rights efforts as well as in the Mississippi Freedom Democrats challenge in Atlantic City. Although we hadn't been introduced earlier, I had seen him several times and he seemed to know quite a bit about me. He emphasized that I should avoid the kinds of confrontations that might lead to arrest, especially during the weeks leading up to the election.

"If the police hassle you," he said, "just do as they say without any back talk. We want you to keep that lovely smile just the way it is." Since I had suffered when younger from the feeling that my teeth were too big, I was pleased to note that his were as large as mine and his smile was gorgeous. He also asked me to try to get Washington CORE to sponsor me with a small stipend, since the amount SNCC would pay me would not be enough to defeat a charge of vagrancy in Mississippi.

"The more effective you are, the more Mr. Charlie will try to sideline you," Courtland said. "Other CORE chapters are chipping in to keep our workers from being jailed as vagrants and DC CORE can well afford to do the same." When we finished talking business, he asked me about some movement people in DC and I asked about Fannie Lou Hamer. Courtland said she was probably working hard for freedom in Ruleville, Mississippi. "But she could be anywhere. She never lets up! I'll see that she learns you're here. I know it'll make her happy."

A young, light-skinned black man with a large forehead, cool to spare, and the romantic name of Ivanhoe, drove me to a bus station, not Trailways, and waited with me until I boarded a bus for Moss Point. Through my open window, I watched with dismay as a policeman approached him after he turned to leave. I pulled my head back into deeper shadow and raised a hand to my cheek when it got through to me that Ivanhoe was telling the policeman he had just put his sister on the bus. As the bus began slowly to back away from the loading dock, the policeman looked from Ivanhoe to me and back again. Ivanhoe waved and I did too, effectively blocking the policeman's view until the bus turned and I was on my way.

Passing through Hattiesburg and more than a score of smaller towns, I was glad to see that, unlike in the North, blacks and whites frequently appeared to be living side by side. It was disquieting, however, to see so many pickup trucks with gun racks bristling with weapons and bumpers plastered with Confederate flags and sometimes the words "COON HUNTER." Rolling through large tracts of pine forest toward the finish of a trip that had begun in DC, I brooded that I might have taken myself so far out of my element that I wouldn't be able to find my way back. I was not an inexperienced Gretel who could be beguiled by gingerbread forms, but I was a city person who as a girl had loathed "the country life," associating it with dispirited confinement in a dirt cellar during two years in hiding. After the war, when my father had sent me to the countryside to improve my health, which had been impaired by tuberculosis masquerading as smoke poisoning or vice versa, I had threatened suicide.

After a long, flat glide through marshlands, past sawmills and stubbled fields, the bus finally arrived at Moss Point, a sun-bleached hamlet of wooden houses, stores, and churches no more than two or three stories high. A few pine trees cast long shadows beneath pink-tinted clouds. Dust like finely powdered blood was everywhere. Waiting for me at the tiny bus station was Mrs. Parker, a large, middle-aged woman with a penetrating look and such imposing dignity that I imagined she must be descended from African queens. With her was Tilmon McKeller, an SNCC worker whose manner and movements had the understated grace of a mischievous brown bear. I had first met Tilmon in Atlantic City and was glad to be greeted by a familiar face. He seemed pleased to see me, too, but anxious, as project director, to appear disciplined and in command of the situation.

As we drove from the bus depot in a dented Oldsmobile, Tilmon asked me what I had been told in Jackson, then he let Mrs. Parker fill me in on local priorities, the top of the list being a concerted effort to register people to vote in the election on November third. My Freedom School in Pascagoula would be an important part of the campaign, she said. We also wanted to integrate local schools and get Moss Point to hire a Negro policeman, she added, pinching my arms, ribs, and legs. Because she obviously had X-ray vision, I didn't protest or even flinch as she poked and squeezed to find out how much, if any, flesh covered my bones. Tilmon repeated Courtland Cox's admonition to forget about any form of civil disobedience until after the election. I tried to assure him that I had no desire to go to jail." Tomorrow," Mrs. Parker pointed out, "is Constitution Day. We're going to the high school assembly in the morning so you can tell the young people their parents have to get registered. Then we're going to the African Baptist Church to fix it so you can tell the congregation on Sunday that Jesus wants them to reddish." Having learned from Lou Smith that many Mississippians deliberately said "reddish" when they meant register, I understood what Mrs. Parker wanted me to do. And today is Yom Kippur, the Day of Atonement, I thought, and I'm not registered, myself. Worse, I'm not a Baptist or a Christian or even a believer. I was almost dizzy from fatigue and the strain of following strange accents, and was beginning to feel distressed by the prospect of being a religious hypocrite. I knew this might be part of the job, but it made me uncomfortable.

Tilmon tactfully filled the silence created by my failure to respond to Mrs. Parker, informing me that we were on our way to Mama Scott's house. He said the Scotts were an elderly couple who strongly supported the movement and had volunteered to take me into their home. He added that I would be the first white civil rights worker in Moss Point to live with a Negro family.

"Mama Scott will take good care of you," Mrs. Parker said. "She'll put some meat on those bones."

Feeling immediately less tired, I asked where the whites who had participated in the Summer Project had lived. Tilmon said most of them had rented motel rooms or apartments. I began to feel suffused with pleasure at the prospect of living with the elderly couple, especially Mama Scott. It would be like having a grandmother again, a private victory over the Nazis who had taken mine away from me.

We stopped before an unpainted wooden house, standing alone on stone pilings in a patch of yard with beds of flowers, herbs, and a few old trees. As we got out of the car, the door of the house opened and a large, gray-haired woman came outside. She descended two steps and stood in front of the house, smiling, while a tall man wearing khaki trousers and a white shirt quietly filled the doorway. I walked over to Mrs. Scott and was enfolded in bare arms larger than Fannie Lou Hamer's and as strong if not stronger. As she held me, the tension from two sleepless nights and days disappeared.

"Welcome, child, welcome!" Mrs. Scott said. "We've been waiting for you!"

I loved her immediately. I've never put much faith in love at first sight, although it must work out for some, but I can often tell by the way I am held or touched how I will feel about a person for the rest of my life, and so it was with Mama Scott. And I wasn't in the least put off by Mr. Scott's amused reserve. The quiet assurance with which he offered me his home conveyed good will as well as a strong sentinel commitment.

Mama Scott showed me my room, which had a high wrought-iron bed covered with quilts in contrasting colors and designs. Beside the bed stood a small dresser that doubled as a night table and near the window was a cherry rocker that looked perfect for a nursing mother. A hooked rug that was somewhat faded but freshly washed lay beside the bed on a dark floor made of ordinary planks in varying widths and lengths. I felt privileged to have been given such a room.

Asked what I would like for dinner, I said that what I wanted most urgently was a bath. Mama Scott took me into the bathroom, which had brass fixtures that reminded me of some I had known in Europe. She said that Tilmon and Mrs. Parker were staying for dinner but that I needn't hurry, since dinner would be ready when I was finished, not before.

After filling an ancient tub with cool water to draw the feverish Mississippi heat from my skin, I soaked and soaped away the dust, and floated and relaxed my limbs until there was no more need. Then I pulled the plug, stood up, took a towel from the wall rack at the foot of the tub, and began to dry off, closing my eyes to enjoy the feel of textured dry cloth against my skin. Very soon, however, my body began to tingle strangely. Coming out of my reverie, I looked down and saw that my legs, waist, and breasts were covered with swiftly crawling creatures. An army of small black ants! The towel, too, was teeming with them, and as I watched, petrified, they streamed across my hands and arms to other parts of my body. Wanting desperately to scream, I constricted my throat to keep from betraying that I was terrified, becoming hysterical, and completely undone. SNCC had taught me how to react to epithets, assault, arrest, even cattle prods, but nothing had prepared me for an ant attack.

About to start crying, I saw myself reflected in the mirror above the sink. From the expression on my face and the way I held the towel, I was reminded of the DAR woman who hadn't wanted to give me my certificate of citizenship. Despite my panic, I laughed, almost but not quite hysterically, and immediately dropped into the remaining water, then submerged and thrashed about until I had washed all my tormentors down the drain.

I didn't mention the ants at dinner, or ever after. Mama Scott and Mrs. Parker were pleased that someone so skinny could have such a large appetite. I was hungry, and I remembered my husband's taunt that I would not last because I didn't like southern cooking.

There was an aftershock the next morning, however, when I came into the kitchen for breakfast. The bread had been precisely tunneled by what could only have been a hungry mouse. After I convinced Mama Scott that I was still full from the night before, I sat with her, happily sipping a cup of coffee spiked with chicory while planning what to say to the high school students. While I was musing about this, Mr. Scott silently set before me a plate of fried bananas sprinkled with powdered sugar. I made myself try a bite, and then delightedly devoured the rest.

Chapter Eight

Freedom Ways

I managed to carry out Mrs. Parker's first-day assignments without visibly embarrassing her. The children seemed surprised but pleased when I criticized the Constitution on Constitution Day for having permitted slavery. Their teachers apparently had treated the founding document as being above reproach, like the Holy Bible, which also condoned slavery. But afterward, the head teacher thanked me for making the point and thanked Mrs. Parker for bringing me.

At the Baptist church, a raspy-voiced minister asked me what I planned to tell the congregation on Sunday. Lacking a plan, I told him I would say that I was a Jew born in Nazi Germany and that I had come to America to find freedom, but had found that many people here aren't free. I said I would remind them that the Israelites of old had crossed the Red Sea without a boat to get their freedom, and I would suggest that the voter registration office was their Red Sea to cross. This seemed to go over well enough. At least Mrs. Parker seemed satisfied. But after I spoke on Sunday, I discovered that some of the congregation thought I was still a teenager.

Four of us worked out of the COFO office in tiny Moss Point, which was about ten miles from the Gulf of Mexico, in the southeast corner of Mississippi. From Mama Scott's house, the office was a fifteen-minute walk alongside a shaded swamp that made me remember the three civil rights workers whose bodies had been found a few weeks earlier under a newly constructed earthen dam. Although they had been killed a hundred miles away, an earthen dam sounded to me like something that would be located on the edge of a swamp. When possible, I timed my walk to work to avoid the boisterous arrival of youths at a white school across the street from the office. The looks and curled-lip comments of students as they passed our office told me not to risk close encounters with them. Seeing some of them through the office window while I was writing a letter to Daniel, I told him how discouraging it was to think that they might become Mississippi's leaders.

Despite the persistent violence against rights workers, fear was not always uppermost on my mind. It could be pushed deep into my brain stem by feelings of joy, love, or anger, or by the mental exertion demanded by a complex task, such as teaching someone twice my age how to read and write. But it was always there, somewhere in the shadows, even when I felt most secure. And Daniel and close friends far away also felt it, as I was reminded by Martin Puryear, the DC artist whom Daniel and I had persuaded to join the Peace Corps instead of the army. Living alone in a primitive hut in the interior of Sierra Leone, Martin wrote to say how concerned he was for my safety.

To keep my cool, I would sometimes remind myself that, as much as I wanted to avoid becoming a victim, I would rather be a victim than a victimizer; also, that I had lived with worse fears as a child, including the dreadful one that I might do something that might cause my mother to be killed. It seemed to me in Mississippi that local whites were less comfortable with themselves than Nazi Germans had been. I knew that there were killers among them, but in public the locals seemed more prone to bluff and bravado than Germans, and easily frightened of people, even children, who posed no real threat. Perhaps the contradiction of practicing oppression while preaching freedom weakened their conviction. Blacks, who had much more to fear, seemed less self-conscious, though stressed by the need to read whites' minds that were governed more by racism than reason. Much as I believed in nonviolence and gun control, I was not unhappy that Mr. Scott slept with a revolver under his pillow and a loaded shotgun nearby. I knew that his weapons were only for self-defense, and I was glad he was prepared.

There had been a dozen or more people working out of the COFO office in Moss Point during Freedom Summer, but when I arrived there were only three other SNCC workers, the other organizations in the council having lost or reassigned their workers when the summer volunteers went home. In addition to Tilmon, our chief, who was from Louisiana, there was a younger black man from Mississippi, who had a wagonload of charm, and a young white woman, a summer volunteer from Wisconsin, who had fallen in love with him. It didn't take me long to get over Carol's Germanic appearance, blond and fair, and realize that she wasn't naive, but was too courageous to back away from the difficulties posed by an interracial marriage. As for our two black male colleagues, they were as different from one another as Carol and I were from each other. Tilmon was reserved, thoughtful but not very communicative, deliberately cool, while the young swain was quick to smile and eager to please.

Although still in my twenties, I was the oldest, and one of the very few married women working as SNCC field staff. What bound us together was our determination to fight injustice in Mississippi, no matter what. I had been there at least a month when a white volunteer arrived, dressed in a suit and tie. He was obviously a spy, but Tilmon more or less accepted him because he had a car that, unlike ours, was in good repair and would not be impounded from time to time by the police. We did our best to keep important or sensitive information out of his sight.

The summer volunteers and rights workers had done an outstanding job of organizing support for the Mississippi Freedom

Democratic Party, which challenged the all-white delegation in Atlantic City. Our task was to turn that energy into real votes in the upcoming national and local elections. Usually working in pairs, we canvassed door to door in and around Moss Point and neighboring hamlets, and in Pascagoula, the much larger shipbuilding center on the Gulf. We attempted to allay fears of white reprisal by pointing out that the Justice Department had brought a lawsuit that had put Mississippi's unfair election procedures under a federal spotlight. Some registrars had been ordered to make radical changes in eligibility requirements that were used to disqualify African Americans. Because of this suit, we said, there was a much greater chance now that an attempt to register would be successful. We offered instruction and other assistance to anyone who wished it and encouraged people to discuss misgivings with us and with family and friends.

Those who were prevented from registering for the officially recognized election were encouraged to participate in the unofficial but color-blind Freedom Vote that would begin earlier and conclude on the day before the official election. The Freedom Vote would demolish the racialists' myth that African Americans wouldn't vote even if they had the chance. It would also spotlight the candidates they supported. Two leaders of the Freedom Democratic Party were running in both elections, Aaron Henry for the US Senate seat held by John Stennis and Victoria Gray for the US House of Representatives. Talking with people who had never been allowed to vote, I was repeatedly impressed and sometimes humbled by their knowledge of the issues and the historical forces at play in these elections.

One of my first assignments was to help Mrs. Parker persuade a local minister to make his church available for voter-registration classes and meetings. It was not a request to be considered lightly. A few months earlier, racists had fired into a building in the area that was being used for a civil rights meeting. A young woman in the building had been shot in the stomach and severely injured. A group of African Americans in a car had seen the attack and had followed the assailants. But when they tried to report the assault they were the ones arrested, and the shooters remained free. Under the circumstances, the minister, in my opinion, could be forgiven if he hesitated to expose his parishioners to similar outrages. Mrs. Parker was a bulwark of the church, however, and she didn't need any help from me to overcome hesitation; she could do it alone. When she made it clear that she and others would withdraw from the congregation if he refused, the pastor consented. His cooperation proved contagious, and soon most of the local black clergy were enthusiastic about participating in the coming elections.

The two issues the black community seemed to feel strongest about were school integration and the hiring of a black policeman. Ten years after the Supreme Court mandated integration "with all deliberate speed," Moss Point, like most of the South, continued to segregate schoolchildren. Many African Americans in the community threatened to boycott all-black schools unless there was progress, but whites delayed for several more years, occasionally offering concessions such as more used textbooks for black students, before finally allowing a few courageous black children through the door. As for the need for a black policeman, Mrs. Parker explained that police indifference to crimes against black people was a galling problem.

"Unless we're minding their children or cooking their dinner, they don't care a damn what happens to us," she said.

"The trouble is that they're too busy busting SNCC workers," Tilmon joked. However, he and the rest of the staff strongly supported the demand. I was enthusiastic because I felt the wrath of a white policeman my first week in Moss Point, when I used the "colored" toilet facilities at the local fairgrounds. Until that moment, it had been with pure delight that I experienced a Mississippi fair—it reminded me of the Hamburg DOM, a huge festival or funfair I used to go to in Germany, the only place my father let his daughters indulge themselves without restraint. So until my choice of restrooms so infuriated a white policeman that he literally climbed my frame, I was blissfully enjoying myself. The clash, however, was immediate and forceful. The policeman grabbed my shoulders and shook me violently as he berated me for "using the Nigger shithouse." Fortunately, one of his colleagues intervened, making him let me go and then pushing him out of range.

Mrs. Parker was jubilant when a city official finally deigned to give her an audience a few days after the incident at the fairground. Afterward, all of us felt elated because the official had asserted that "a Nigger policeman might come in handy" and that the city would probably have to integrate its schools if the Democrats won the upcoming election. Not long after the official's conciliatory words to Mrs. Parker, I became aware that people were referring to me as "little Nigger." I understood this to be an affectionate use of the "N" word, which they sometimes used themselves but deeply resented when whites used it. I had noticed earlier that nonwhite Mississippians preferred the word "Negro" when referring to people of color, and were not comfortable with "black" or "blacks." So I refrained from identifying people as black and instead used Negro and Negroes when appropriate.

Proper word usage wasn't a big problem within the movement, where black was beginning to replace Negro, but I raised it at an SNCC conference in Pass Christian, a town at the other end of Mississippi's Gulf Coast. At the time we were under siege. Telephone lines had been cut and armed patrols in pickup trucks circled the building, training their spotlights on exits and cutting off all access to the highway. Now and then a shot was fired, but no police came. We slept on the floor in a corridor, afraid to walk past the windows.

I raised the what's-in-a-name non-issue to change the conversation from tales of beatings, shootings, and other terrors, which had the baffling effect of causing my colleagues to slap hands or bump shoulders and roar with laughter. They didn't, however, laugh about atrocities such as the assassination of Medgar Evers in Jackson, Mississippi. To those present who had known him, Evers's death had been like losing an older brother or favorite uncle. For several people at the conference, belief in nonviolence as an effective means to a desired end had perished with him in June of 1963. Others had lost their faith three months later when four children in a Birmingham Sunday school were killed, or two months before the conference when the tortured bodies of civil rights workers James Chaney, Michael Schwerner, and Andrew Goodman were found a few hours away from where we were now besieged. At the beginning of the conference, there was a lot of talk about those murders and about David Dennis, CORE's top official in Mississippi, who had delivered the eulogy at Chaney's funeral, which had to be separate from the other two because Mississippi wouldn't allow blacks and whites to be buried together. Dennis was not only aggrieved by the deaths, he was furious with federal and state governments for not even trying to protect rights workers or effectively punish their killers. At the funeral, he questioned whether nonviolence could be effective against unremitting violence. Since no one had been arrested for these murders, I and everyone else at the conference was aware, though we didn't say so, that the killers might be among those brandishing guns outside our doors and windows.

Whether they continued to believe in nonviolence or not, everyone at the conference was angry about the lack of justice for blacks and their allies. Several among us had suffered severe abuse while in police custody. Larry Guyot, my boss as the head of the SNCC-COFO district office in Hattiesburg, was a case in point. I first met Larry at the conference, but I had heard about him from Fannie Lou Hamer. While returning from a voting rights seminar in another state, she and another woman, Annell Ponder, were arrested and then brutally beaten in the Winona, Mississippi, jail. Larry was sent to investigate and upon his arrival, he was hit repeatedly by a state trooper who then handed him over to local men who beat him mercilessly.

They hit him in the face so many times that his eyes swelled shut and there was a danger he might end up blind. Although I let him know I had talked with Ms. Hamer on the bus from Atlantic City, I didn't ask Larry about the beatings but about the way that many local African Americans disliked being referred to as black. Since he was not only my boss but also a black Mississippian who had been in the movement there since its early days, I thought he would be the one to reconcile local attitudes with SNCC's desire for people to recognize that black is beautiful. I asked him how I should deal with this apparent dichotomy.

He frowned and stroked his chin, looking like a young actor portraying a prophet in a biblical drama, then let a mischievous smile crease his cheeks.

"By example," he said. "If you show people that you truly believe black is beautiful, that should do the trick."

This sounded to me a bit suggestive, bordering on double entendre. If so, it was double-edged. Stokely Carmichael's comment at an earlier planning session, that "the position of women in the movement should be prone," had not been taken seriously at this conference, but no man made fun of a woman's complaint that men who talk black should sleep black. Larry didn't know that I knew his girlfriend or fiancée, and I didn't tell him or respond to his answer to my question. I simply smiled back and we enjoyed a casual discussion of emotionally-weighted words and unexpected reactions to them. Getting past the truism that a gem on one tongue may be gravel on another, we reflected contentedly on the dangers and delights of ironic speech, especially on the topic of race. Everybody in SNCC adored Stokely and even the women insisted that he had been joking and trying to shock with his comment that we should be prone, but Larry conceded that the remark resonated because many young men endorsed it.

Giving only mild examples, Larry averred that some of the brothers' obscene sounding off or signifying to one another, often in rhyme, had a lot in common with solo jazz riffs. The younger brother of our mutual friend Ed Brown was cited as an exemplar.

"I didn't know Rap was in Mississippi," I said. "The last I heard he had been shot in Cambridge, Maryland, and was still there."

"He comes down sometimes to be with Ed," Larry replied, "and to get away from those crazies in Maryland. I ran into him the last time I was in Jackson."

We agreed that only a few white people could appreciate Rap's verbal pyrotechnics and that the everyday language of mild-mannered activists such as Lou Smith would outrage most white people because of his frequent use of "motherfucker." As we talked about the dangers of ironic comments being taken literally, especially by those who wanted to discredit the speaker's other positions, I pointed out that Hannah Arendt, a German Jew who hated the Nazis, had been pilloried for her ironic comment that Eichmann was Zionist since he wanted to ship Jews to Palestine. However, we both agreed that she should have understood that this would offend. Blacks can say terrible things to one another, and often do, Guyot observed, but when a comment like Stokely's or Arendt's is aired publicly, it can haunt the person forever.

Thinking about the communications difficulties of Hannah Arendt, who was a famous scholar, reminded me that Tilmon had given me a key to a house in Pascagoula that I was supposed to turn into a Freedom School. I told Larry that I was excited about the assignment, but I repeated the warning I had given in Jackson about my never having taught school before.

"That was true for many people this past summer," Larry said, "but it worked out fine. What was your major?

"Child Psychology."

"Great! In my book that's better than Education. It's a damn sight better than Sociology."

I promised to do my best. "My real interest is art," I added. "I liked studying psychology, but I couldn't hack working in the children's ward at Bellevue. The children needed love, and they weren't getting it."

"I doubt if I could have taken that either," Larry said, "but don't worry. With psychology, art, and a good heart, you'll do fine. How are you at music?"

"I love it, and I've learned some great songs since I've been here. But I don't know enough to teach it."

"Let the kids teach you."

That night I wrote to publishing houses, the Library of Congress, the United Federation of Teachers (New York's teachers' union), and anyone else I thought might help me with the Freedom School.

Chapter Nine

Freedom Cross

On the way home from Pass Christian, after the siege was lifted as suddenly as it had materialized, I drove the Moss Point contingent's battered Oldsmobile. I had been given this responsibility because I drove fast and had a clean record as a driver. One of the ways Mississippi police restricted the mobility of rights workers was to charge us with real or bogus traffic violations. I had been warned in Jackson that if a policeman took my license and told me to follow him to the station, I would likely be charged with driving without a license if I complied. The fine was stiff but not as severe as getting knocked in the head and charged with resisting arrest if one refused. On that night, however, we passed through Gulfport and Biloxi without a problem. Carol and I were in the front and the men were sitting low in the back seat. We had a good start, but by the time we reached Ocean Springs, we were riding on empty, so I pulled off the road when I saw a sign for gasoline.

The place we stopped at was a beer joint with a pink neon sign that announced "EATS" and a smaller blue one that indicated there were pool tables inside. Not wanting to leave the car, I beeped the horn twice. A middle-aged attendant wearing jeans and a T-shirt with a cigarette pack rolled in one sleeve came out and proceeded to comply with my request for five bucks' worth of regular gas. He put the pump nozzle into the car's gas port, but then, oddly, went back into the tavern. As we waited for the tank to fill, we looked at the many pickup trucks with gun racks parked near the building. Tilmon told me to start the engine, which I did, and seconds later, more than half a dozen white men rushed out the tavern door and headed toward our car. I didn't need further instruction. I put the car in gear and floored the accelerator pedal, throwing loose gravel behind us and enveloping our pursuers in a dust cloud that smelled of burnt rubber. I had to drive on the shoulder of the road for several seconds before rocketing back onto the asphalt roadway.

We didn't reenter the speed limit until we turned left ten miles later, so as to lose any pursuers, and approached Moss Point via a federal highway north of the town. Then, just before the interstate, Tilmon asked me to pull over. He got out of the car and removed from our gas port the curved metal nozzle with a bit of hose attached that had been ripped from the gasoline pump. He held it up in the car lights and pretended to spray the windshield with it. All of us got out of the car to examine it, and then we doubled over in laughter. Finally, Tilmon took the wheel and an hour later dropped me off at Mrs. Scott's house.

Because I was impatient and Tilmon didn't like to be rushed, it was three days before we went to Pascagoula to look at the schoolhouse. Once there, I saw that it was a one-story box with a slightly pitched roof and outside walls covered by white asbestos siding. It stood in a green patch within a residential neighborhood of similar houses and patches. There were two large rooms, a bathroom, and a small kitchen. It also had a weathered wooden front porch with a roof supported by warped four-by-fours. I attacked the interior with a broom, a mop, some rags, and soap and water while he swept and picked up outside. Afterward we painted "FREEDOM SCHOOL" in large black letters on the white siding, and then left to seek the support of local ministers.

Enrollment in the school exceeded just about everybody's expectations. Within a week or so, I had around two dozen elementary-school children coming on a more or less regular basis. Half a dozen adults also came to learn how to read and write. I painted slogans, such as "ONE MAN ONE VOTE" and "FREEDOM NOW," all over the dreadful siding on the front of the house, and people from other places began to drop by for a visit or drive by for a look. A newspaper boy who was white began to deliver the local paper free of charge and ran errands for me. He asked a lot of questions about the school and pleaded with me to let him attend. I thought it would be great to have him, especially since we were demanding compliance with the Supreme Court's ten-year-old ruling to integrate schools. COFO headquarters in Jackson agreed, but said I had to have the written consent of both of the boy's parents, which proved to be impossible because the boy's father was a staunch segregationist. Although the boy didn't attend the school, he continued, secretly, to do things for me. One morning people in Pascagoula's more affluent neighborhoods awoke to find that someone had put up posters urging them to vote for Lyndon B. Johnson, Aaron Henry, and Victoria Gray.

In addition to teaching in the Freedom School and electioneering, I met with black workers at the shipyards in Pascagoula, which struck me as a semi-tropical version of Hamburg harbor's vaunted shipbuilding and repair facilities for ocean liners and warships. The workers told me that their union represented whites and blacks differently, with black workers getting short-changed on seniority, promotions, and access to good jobs. According to Daniel, the National Labor Relations Board should not have allowed this, but apparently it was responsive to local political pressures. I also met with workers at a chemical plant who said they were compelled to work overtime without getting paid time-and-a-half. Daniel wrote that this would be illegal if they were covered by federal wage and hour laws. He sent me relevant information and contacted Don Slaiman, the head of the civil rights unit at the AFL-CIO, and Norman Hill, a former CORE official who worked with him. They put me in touch with an AFL-CIO official who lived in Pascagoula, cautioning that I must use an untapped phone to contact him and mustn't let anyone know about our connection. Even if the workers had a good legal position, that wasn't enough in Mississippi, they said, but perhaps the local union official could advise us how best to proceed.

The success of the school or possibly my efforts with shipyard workers, or both, aroused the ire of the Ku Klux Klan or its suit-and-tie alter ego, the White Citizens' Councils. One sunlit morning I arrived at the school to find a large, charred, still-smoldering cross planted in the front yard. For a moment I sat in the car, transfixed by the sight of this Christian symbol being used as a weapon of hate. Then I shuddered, remembering the stark black Hakenkreuz (hooked cross or swastika) displayed everywhere by the Nazis to convey a similar message. "What will this do to my children?" I asked aloud, but more to myself than to Tilmon, who was cursing quietly but steadily, as if reciting an incantation to dispel the power of the thing in front of us.

"Some of them will have seen it on the way to school," he said. "Everybody will know about it by now."

"We'll have to help them see what a stupid trick this is," I said.

"How are you going to do that?" he asked. "A lot of people take this sort of thing seriously."

"Maybe I'll put a jack-o'-lantern on top of it. But I want to make it a teaching tool, so the kids will see it as a misuse of the cross by people stupid enough to think it will frighten us."

"You're not frightened?"

"If I am, I'm not going to tell anybody. In a way, this validates our being here. We need a school to counteract this bullshit. I may just paint 'bullshit' on the cross."

Tilmon winced, and then he said, "Maybe that's not such a bad idea!" He said it in such a way that we were both able to laugh. Aware that others were probably looking, we walked past the cross as if it were no more frightening than a Halloween pumpkin. After checking out the building to make sure nothing was amiss inside, he went back to Moss Point.

Before the children arrived, I doused the top of the cross with water and, after the surface seemed dry enough, I took a brush and a can of white paint and painted the word "FREEDOM" on the crosspiece. I let the children talk about the cross until it had been substantially demystified. Then I told them that the people who had burned the cross were trying to frighten us and asked if they had done so. "No way!" the children replied. "No way!" After they went home, many brought their parents back to look.

Instead of scaring people away from the school, the freedom cross attracted more students, adults as well as children. As word spread, people came from other towns and cities to see and to photograph it. The children liked to form a circle around their cross and sing freedom songs. To keep it from being carted away at night, I would get some of the larger kids to help me take it inside. In the morning, I would sometimes lean it against the wall outside on the porch. Wherever it was placed, it was a stinging riposte to the Klan.

I don't think the union contact Don Slaiman had provided knew about the cross, but he was clearly nervous about the Klan. He wanted to know where I was calling from and whether I had given his name or number to anyone else. I tried to assure him that everything was fine, but didn't really succeed. He said he was sorry but that it would be impossible for him to meet with me or with the black workers. He told me they had to convince the National Labor Relations Board (NLRB) and the Wage-Hour Administration to act. When I said they couldn't get a foot in NLRB's door, he promised to get back to me with two contacts: one a savvy union organizer in the chemical industry and the other a lawyer in the office of the NLRB's general counsel. About a week later he gave me the names and numbers he had promised and I passed them on to the workers.

Chapter Ten

Mississippi, Mon Amour

It was exhilarating to be so involved in the struggle to combat centuries of racial subjugation. Like others, I had volunteered for the task in Mississippi because I believed that Mississippi was where the need was greatest, where oppression was a way of life and a frequent cause of death. Perhaps because of what had been done to my family and others like them, I felt that the cause of African Americans was mine also and that I owed it to my past and to our mutual future to intervene. But if I had been moved to come to Mississippi mainly by feelings of anger and duty, these were soon replaced by the somewhat delirious feelings of an affair of the heart.

Yes, I missed my husband and three-year-old son; in fact, missed them more and more every day. Lying on my side I missed the feel of Daniel's shoulder beneath my cheek and his slightly hairy chest beneath my arm. That was my rightful place, the place where I basked in his love and he in mine, and we in ours for our son. It was a place of arousal—we never wore pajamas—as well as relaxation, of dreams and somber reflection, contentment and deep yearning, even tears. It was my one most special place and I missed it.

What's more, I was even more in love with Daniel now than when the bogus Dr. Black pronounced us husband and wife. In Mississippi, it was sunshine clear that Daniel's trust was my most valuable asset. I thought I was probably the only SNCC worker then in Mississippi who had left a toddler and loving husband at home. I had come knowing that many people there and even a few in DC would say that I should have stayed at home and must be out for sexual adventure. Neither accusation bothered me, although I knew the importance of denying evil-thinkers ammunition. Both Daniel and I understood that racism is harmful to all children and wanted to be able to look ours in the eye when he asked later on what we had done to oppose it. Given my experience with the racial genocide that would later be called the Holocaust, which few SNCC workers knew much about and, so far as I knew, none had shared, I probably would have gone to Mississippi even if Daniel had insisted that it was too dangerous, but it was my good fortune to have his full support.

Each morning I awoke excited by the challenges that lay ahead, and each day I became more attached to the people I lived and worked with. I loved them for the dangers they had passed as well as for the content of their character. I adored their cool as they invoked the wrath of Mr. Charlie, their stubborn dignity in the face of intimidation and derision, their deft skewering of pretensions and their irrepressible humor before, after, and even during a confrontation. But most of all I loved them for their warmth and openness to me, for sharing their vulnerability as well as their strength, and for allowing me to nest in their affections.

In my expanded emotional state, I wrote to Daniel, telling him that I had been "seduced by an intangible," and was suffering from "a disease called Mississippi." I said it was "a seduction of the mind," but that "every third day I have a minute of lucidity in which I see Mississippi as it is." I also wrote that I saw the law as the oppressor, and that "the KKK holds its meetings in police stations." I confessed that I feared that I would not escape from Mississippi even if I left it, since "I have Mississippi in my blood, and the disease has taken hold." But "freedom will provide a cure," I continued, and we would see a new day of honor and dignity "when a man no longer has to be afraid but can be a man in every sense of the word." I waxed feverish about our need to succeed, saying that "it is only through Mississippi and because of her that we will change America into what it can and should be."

As a former southerner, Daniel worried constantly about my safety, but was never less than fully supportive. He conveyed no hint of reproach or discouragement, but assured me that he and Danny were doing fine and were getting considerable help from friends, especially from our dear friend Bernice Hooks, who made sure Danny received hands-on maternal affection by taking him into her extended family on many weekends. My mother, however, responded to my letters with brief notes saying that I should return at once to my husband and child, where I belonged. Although I did not doubt that she was concerned for my safety, her tone made it clear that she believed I was shirking my basic duty as a wife, albeit for a laudable cause.

Quite a bit before the end of my sojourn in Mississippi, I began to worry more about leaving the people I had come to work among than about the hazards or the difficulties we faced together. I had accepted their openness and trust as gifts, knowing that the day would come when I would have to leave, but believing that this would not pose a great difficulty. In time, however, I learned that many of the children and adults who frequented the Freedom School had come to believe that I would choose to remain indefinitely and would be joined by my husband and child. I tried to disabuse them of such beliefs, saying I hoped to return with my son for a Christmas visit and would try to return the next year for a few months. But I didn't manage to dislodge the growing conviction that I would remain in Mississippi permanently. I wrote Liz Fusco, COFO's director of the Freedom School program, about my concerns and I also wrote Daniel and explained that I couldn't come home until a replacement was found. Liz, who had been instrumental in getting my school "adopted" by a church group in Pennsylvania, was sympathetic and promised to do her best to find a replacement. She was also concerned about my safety, since I was the only person manning the Pascagoula office and school. She urged me to try to find an adult volunteer to stay with me. Despite her promise and warning, however, I continued to be more concerned by the prospect that people would feel betrayed when I left than I was about my safety. Listening to the children sing freedom songs at the end of a school day, I wondered how I could possibly leave them.

I continued to derive tremendous satisfaction from the school and my relationships until the afternoon when I received a phone call telling me to shut down the school. The call was not totally unexpected. It must have been infuriating, even humiliating, for Klansmen to see their cross become an icon of resistance.

Earlier in the day I had begun to think it might be their day for revenge when I realized that the same car had been making slow circuits around our block throughout the morning. I couldn't see the driver clearly but it looked like a woman, and I told myself there was no reason to connect her behavior to the school. I was more concerned by a pickup truck, driven by a man, that passed in front with less regularity. So I was pleased at first that a woman responded when I stopped teaching to answer the phone. Having received crank calls before, I was about to say "You have the wrong number" and hang up, but I was stopped by the chillingly cultivated tone and language of the caller. She said that I had ignored their warnings and flouted their traditions for much too long, and they were not going to allow a subversive alien to poison the minds of Negro children any longer. She said men were coming to shut me up and shut the school down permanently.

I didn't think the woman was bluffing, but even if I had I wouldn't have risked keeping the children with me. I told them that I had to close the school and that I wanted them to go home and do homework or memorize a poem or draw me a picture and bring it with them tomorrow. If anybody needed a book, I said, they could take one of the thousands of copies of *Amy Vanderbilt's Complete Book of Etiquette* that I had received from its publisher—the only publisher to respond to my appeal for teaching materials. I had so many copies that I was able to make room dividers of them by stacking them on the floor. But as soon as the last child had gone, I began to regret that I hadn't gone home with one of them or at least sent a message to a parent to let someone know what was going on.

Because SNCC's phone bills had become larger than the organization could afford, it had installed pay phones in all its offices, and I discovered after I was alone that I had used up all my change earlier in the day. I couldn't even reach an operator or call the police without a coin. I searched every conceivable place where I might have put one, but found nothing. Not wanting to abandon the school and not having any transportation anyway, I had little choice but to wait and hope that Tilmon would come early to pick me up or someone with change would drop by for a visit.

I tried to write a letter to take my mind off the emergency but nothing worked. After a time, the phone rang again. It was the same woman. "I warned you," she said. Then the phone went dead and I became very frightened. I wanted to hide but there was nowhere to go. I started frantically repositioning the Amy Vanderbilt books, trying to create a protected corner. But after I had walled myself in, I decided that I did not want to be found cowering behind those books. I tumbled the books onto the floor, grabbed a worn-out broom from the kitchen area, and moved toward the entrance. To hell with nonviolence, if anyone came through that door, I was going to swing. I stood there for I don't know how long until I heard the clump of footsteps on the front porch. I retreated a few steps toward the center of the room and stopped.

When Stokely Carmichael rushed into the room followed by Larry Guyot and Tilmon, I went limp all over. In fact, I slowly swooned, and would have fallen to the floor if Stokely hadn't caught me. When I could, I explained what had happened. Stokely said that one of my students had told her mother that I had sent everybody home after receiving several phone calls that seemed to upset me a lot. The mother had called COFO's office in Jackson, which had called Moss Point, where Stokely and Larry were meeting with Tilmon, and they had then hurried to Pascagoula. On the way home to Moss Point, I noticed that Stokely was not wearing an earring. I wanted to ask if he sometimes wore one, but I didn't. The school was not burned down that night and I returned to teach, armed with dimes. In time it was torched, however, and about all that remained were ashy mounds of *Amy Vanderbilt's Complete Book of Etiquette* and a twice-charred cross.

* * *

To boost morale, Tilmon arranged for staff to take an overnight excursion to New Orleans to meet his parents and see the city. Seeing me in a car with three black men, white youths threw rocks at the car as we passed through their neighborhood. This was so unsurprising that it aroused only a few expletives from my companions. Despite the new law banning racial discrimination in places open to the public, the famous French Quarter was still mostly off limits to black men. But Tilmon found us great gumbo and deliciously hot jazz in a black part of town, one as friendly to an integrated group as the Quarter was unfriendly.

A day trip to Mobile, Alabama, to hear Ray Charles was more memorable. Although I had enjoyed some of his recordings, I was not exactly a devotee. In the auditorium, however, I became one as he shared his intense passion for life with every member of the audience. Although local law still mandated separate seating, blacks and whites were soon dancing joyfully together in the aisles. I knew that he had once been chain-whipped on stage for performing to an integrated audience, and I felt that I was honoring his courage by helping to integrate this performance. Instead of being mere entertainment, the concert had the inspiring effect of a Beethoven symphony.

A few weeks before the November elections, the town of Moss Point granted the black community's demand that it hire a black policeman. But this didn't signal a change of heart on the part of white officials. The man they chose was psychopathically opposed to integration and the civil rights movement. Hiring that specific man as a policeman had been a cynically hostile means of punishing that community for the "sin" of pressing for integration. Mrs. Parker, the most outspoken person I knew, was too upset to talk about it. Mr. Scott told me the man was an angry army veteran with a history of mental illness and violence, both of which were well known to the authorities. There were some of course who emphasized the positive, the precedent that had been set, and the possibility that responsibility would rein in the man's temper. But it wasn't long before we realized that, instead, we were in for a reign of terror. Black men who were active in the rights movement were among the first victims. They were brutally clubbed about the head and suffered broken jaws as well as multiple hand, arm, and scalp wounds. Many others in the black community also were beaten for little or no cause. Whites, apparently including Carol and I, did not have to worry about being attacked by him.

Around that time I began to experience occasional difficulty going to sleep. During working hours I remained optimistic that we would somehow succeed in defeating the Jim Crow laws, but lying in my bed at night I would be visited by unwelcome memories that slyly morphed into troubling questions about the future if nonviolence failed. Coming through my bedroom window, the smell of plowed earth and pine boughs made me feel like I was lying on my cot in the frame hut on Frau Pimber's farm outside Hamburg. If a dog barked after I closed my eyes, I instantly recalled cowering in an earthen dugout, expecting the SS to root us out of our hiding place at any moment. Perhaps because Mr. Scott was so well armed, I didn't imagine that hooded Klansmen were crouched outside my bedroom window preparing to ignite a fire bomb, although I and everyone else in Mississippi knew that was a possibility. What kept me awake at night after the appointment of the psychopathic policeman was not so much the fear of an imminent attack as a gathering sense of déjà vu.

I had come to Mississippi with few illusions. The acquittal of Emmett Till's murderers almost ten years earlier had let me know that the state tolerated the murder of black people. The murders of Chaney, Schwerner, and Goodman had demonstrated that the license to kill extended to rights workers. I didn't think that Schwerner and Chaney would still be alive if they hadn't been Jews, but I knew that Jews were on the Klan's hate list and I felt sure that they knew by then that I was a Jew. Recent events, in any case, were making me more conscious of that identity and the power wielded by the Klan and the more openly despicable White Citizens' Council. At the same time I was aware that their power did not allow them to engage in the aggressive genocide I had experienced as a child, and that the rights movement had mounted a positive and fairly effective challenge to their power. In a very personal way, I was fighting back for those who had been powerless and friendless against the Nazis. And I had lots of friends, all of us fighting nonviolently. With these reassuring thoughts and a little moonlight brightening the bedroom, I was able to pretend I was lying on Daniel's shoulder and go to sleep.

Chapter Eleven

Struggle and Flight

There wasn't much time for reflection during the day, as we worked to line up voters for the two upcoming elections. The first one, the Freedom Vote, was conducted by civil rights groups to show that black Mississippians would vote in the second election if they had the opportunity. The first vote was open to just about any adult Mississippian, no matter what color, who cared to cast a ballot. In keeping with our belief in "one man, one vote," registration was as simple and straightforward as the rules for the other election were complex and subject to abuse. To make it as inclusive as possible, the polls would be open for three days. The following day, November 3, 1964, was National Election Day, when most white Mississippians would be allowed to vote in the "official" election, while most African Americans would be shut out because the state had the will and the power to exclude them.

Although the summer volunteers and rights workers had done an excellent job of organizing to challenge Mississippi's all-white delegation to the Democratic Party's convention in Atlantic City, there were many African Americans who didn't see the point of participating in an election if the results didn't actually count. But after the Freedom Party's courageous stand at the convention, many of them saw the light and were ready to cast a ballot to protest the denial of their rights. This was true especially of those who had seen Fannie Lou Hamer "tell it like it is in Mississippi," when she spoke to the convention while national television cameras rolled. If a prospective voter had seen or heard about that event and was still reluctant, I would tell him or her that I had met Ms. Hamer in Atlantic City and had come to Mississippi because she said it was important to prove to people in Washington that whites were lying when they said Negroes didn't care to vote. I didn't need to plead with many people, however, and along with most rights workers in our area was amazed at the turnout for the Freedom Vote. For three days we were so busy taking people to and from the polls and taking ballot boxes to be tallied that we barely had time to pause for a bite to eat. National Election Day was less hectic, but at the end of the day, several of us were still hungry and, for the first time in quite a while, at loose ends.

The closing of the polls brought an abrupt end to a long campaign that had cost precious lives and engaged many people as never before. Suddenly, this phase of the struggle was over. After the last rural voter was driven home, there was nothing to do but await the election returns. We knew the official vote would go to Barry Goldwater, but the Freedom Vote had been a triumph of creative nonviolent resistance to oppression, and several women who had been handing out literature, minding children, transporting voters, and performing other tasks wanted to do something special to mark the occasion. About the only thing open nearby that served food was Burnham Drugstore. Although I believed that it probably wouldn't serve us at its lunch counter, I suggested that we give it a try to see what would happen. Perhaps after the election, someone else said, there would be some federal agency we could complain to if they turned us away. Everyone present was immediately enthusiastic. Since no one wanted to tangle with the new black policeman, said to be in a rage over the unprecedented turnout, it was agreed that we would leave under our own steam if the police were summoned. This being clear, I felt that our escapade wouldn't violate SNCC's ban on sit-ins. So I drove us to the drugstore and parked legally in front.

When we went inside and sat down, the white clerks and counter workers were visibly upset. The other two or three customers got up and stood by the cashier. We examined the menus and discussed the contents among ourselves, but no one made a move to take our order. After several minutes, one of the women in our group told the man behind the counter that we would each like to order a banana split. The man stared at her for several seconds and then said:

"We don't serve Niggers!"

"We didn't ask for Niggers," my companion said. "We want banana splits!"

"Under the new law," another woman said, "you have to serve us."

"After this election," the man replied, "Goldwater's going to tear that law into little pieces. Now, y'all get out of here right now. That includes you!" he added, looking at me. He then told the cashier to "call the police and tell them there's a group of Niggers in the store making trouble and refusing to leave."

"We haven't refused to do anything," my companion said as the cashier made the call. "You're the one who's refusing us."

"Just get your black asses out of here. This counter is closed!"

Feeling that we had scored a victory by keeping our cool while he lost his, we rose from our stools and filed out the door without haste and with heads held high. Once outside, we laughed at our friend's quick-witted response and were glad we had marked the occasion in a manner that would not go unnoticed in Moss Point. But even before everyone was seated in our car, a police car pulled up behind us. Two cops got out and I was glad to see that the black policeman wasn't with them. While one cop went inside for an earful of spleen, the other demanded that I hand over my driver's license and registration, which I did. He looked at the license and asked me my age and date of birth. I told him I would be twenty-nine in two weeks and two days. It took him about a minute, but he finally figured it out, then he put my license in his breast pocket and examined the registration certificate and the plates' front and back. Next he told me to turn on the car lights, which he checked front and back, then to turn on the ignition and hit the brake pedal and use the turn signals. Apparently satisfied, he went to his car and remained there for several minutes. When the other policeman came out of the drugstore, they conferred for a couple of minutes, then my interrogator returned while the other one climbed into the police car. At that point, I began to feel that we might get off without so much as a parking ticket. From the time when I had used the "colored only" toilet at the fairground, I knew that not all Mississippi cops were equally bad.

But instead of giving me back my driver's license, he told me that I was to follow him in my car. He told the others to get out of the car unless they wanted to get arrested. At my urging, all complied. I got out of the car also and approached the officer to ask for my driver's license, causing him to turn on me in a fury.

"Get your ass back in that car before I have it hauled away," he said.

"I just want my license while I follow you," I said. "It's still in your shirt pocket."

"And that's where it stays. I don't know what they tell you Nigger-fuckers in the North, but down here you do what you're told if you want to stay healthy. You hear?"

"Yes sir," I said, recalling CORE's rule to show respect even to an enemy.

When I was booked at the police station, however, I wished that I had withheld the respect. Not only was I charged with driving without a license, but also with disturbing the peace, resisting arrest, and speeding, even reckless and drunken driving. The booking officer had even suggested some of the charges. They were throwing the book at me to make it virtually impossible to plead guilty and pay a small fine or make bail.

Tilmon was there the next day, when I was arraigned and pled not guilty to all charges and waived a preliminary hearing. He told me that SNCC was trying to find a good lawyer to represent me at the trial and I told him that the whole thing was a farce that no real court could take seriously. We both knew, however, that the police would not be making such a fuss if they didn't feel certain they could make something stick. It wasn't really the drugstore incident, which was not a real sit-in, that had set them off, we concluded, but our obvious success in stimulating black participation in political affairs. They were determined to show that such efforts would lead nowhere.

From the first night I was fortunate to have a jail cell to myself. The toilet facilities stank, and there were bugs and rodents galore; however, the food, mainly red beans and rice, was flavorful. The worst part of being incarcerated was lying or sitting on a bunk in the semi-darkness and hearing the pain of others.

Although many SNCC workers, females as well as males, had spent uncontested time in Mississippi's Parchman Farm penitentiary and other hellholes, legal counsel was provided for me by the Lawyers Guild in New Orleans. I hadn't asked for a lawyer and knew little about the Guild except that it had a reputation for defending people like Jack O'Dell. I didn't mind when they said a judge rather than a jury would decide my fate, but wished that I had been allowed more time with the lawyers before the trial. Just as someone said the court was "in session," the trial began, and one of my drugstore companions handed me a carton of cigarettes, which were very welcome since I had been without in jail.

The courtroom was the size of a large classroom and had a long table set a few feet in front of a wall of windows that provided welcome light. The judge, a large man with a faintly pink complexion, was already seated behind the desk when I arrived, escorted by the arresting officers. I was told to take the seat directly across from the judge, whose back was to the windows. My two lawyers sat to my right, at the end of the table, and the two policemen stood behind chairs a few feet away on my left. A white woman I took to be the court stenographer sat to the right of the judge. A state flag hung from a pole near the wall behind the judge. Behind me were rows of chairs occupied by people from the black communities of Moss Point and Pascagoula. I assumed they had been mobilized by Mrs. Parker and others who had participated in the voting drive. The Scotts were sitting in the second row. A few whites looked in from time to time but didn't stay long. Even the whites who worked at the drugstore didn't stick around. Without saying so directly, the police and the judge seemed to want the black community to understand that I was being prosecuted because I was an "outside agitator" who had encouraged local blacks to attempt to order food at the drugstore lunch counter. If the intent was to teach local blacks a lesson, the authorities had an attentive and responsive class. My supporters stayed for the entire length of the trial, which turned out to be several hours, observing and participating like a Greek chorus with audible expressions of dissent or approval, most often a collective sigh or groan.

The two police officers were the main witnesses against me, and my lawyers did an excellent job of exposing the absence of any real evidence to support several of the charges, some of which apparently had been dropped. They had no proof that I had been drinking alcohol other than their assertion that I must have been drunk because I had "gone to the drugstore with a bunch of Niggers and ordered a banana split." After lengthy verbal sparring, the lawyers extracted a virtual admission that the charge of driving without a license was contradicted by the claim that I had resisted arrest by asking for my license as well as by the fact that I was carrying out a police order. They cited cases they said clearly established the right of citizens to disregard normal traffic regulations in obedience to police orders.

At one point the judge, whom the lawyers always treated with the utmost respect, became so irritated with a policeman's fumbling testimony that he took over the narrative and began to describe events that he couldn't have seen even if they had happened.

Because the judge was smoking, I wanted to do the same, but I didn't have any matches and neither did my lawyers. So I would lean across the table that separated us and get a light from the judge, who apparently considered himself a "southern gentleman." As the trial wore on, I began to chain-smoke to calm my nerves, and each time he lit my cigarette there would be an approving hum from the audience, which grew louder each time.

Speaking in my defense, my lawyers said that they were not presenting witnesses because what had happened in the drugstore was not at issue, was not incorporated into any of the charges, and plainly had no bearing on the case. There was, the older lawyer said, no reason for me to testify since I freely admitted the only pertinent facts in evidence, namely that I had fully complied with a policeman's order to follow him. He spoke at length, asserting that the charges were the unfortunate result of "multiple misunderstandings" that stemmed from the excitement generated that day by "the workings of American democracy." It is understandable, he suggested, that after hearing that the nation had embraced radical change, hungry people might go at once to see if this change extended to the soda fountain, "meaning no offense against the peace and dignity of the great state of Mississippi." And it is no wonder, he said, turning toward the most aggressive policeman, who was glowering back at him, that an officer responding to a call after working long hours to maintain order might believe that he needed to act decisively to keep things going smoothly. Concluding his argument, the lawyer insisted that I, a newcomer to this country and this state, had not meant to offend anyone, especially not officers of the law, and that the three nights I had spent in jail were more than enough punishment for any contribution made to these unfortunate misunderstandings.

I understood that the lawyers were trying to give the authorities a graceful line of retreat and that the approach reflected CORE's rules for dealing with adversaries, but I was angry about the ridiculously trumped-up charges and the court's blatant attempts to make them stand up. I wanted the lawyers to say that this was a perversion of justice, or at least be sharply critical rather than everlastingly conciliatory. It occurred to me that Tilmon may have warned them that I might go on the attack if put on the stand or that they simply assumed anyone facing such charges would have a hard time remaining cool. Even in Mississippi it was difficult to bite one's tongue while the people sworn to uphold the law abused it. But when the judge banged the table and said he was ready to pass judgment, the room became absolutely still.

I wasn't surprised that he found me guilty, but when he sentenced me to 180 days in jail, I realized I was in serious trouble. Even then I didn't fully appreciate the gravity of the situation, taking comfort, rather than finding cause for alarm, in the angry response from my supporters. I thought the trial was such a farce that a higher court would surely overturn the ruling. I told Tilmon and the lawyers that I could do the time but that I wanted an appeal all the way to the Supreme Court, if necessary, to expose and repudiate the judge's conduct. After the judge refused to allow an appeal bond, the lawyers said they needed to talk to him in private and get back to me.

The people in the courtroom were quieted by two ministers who were present. As they were leaving, Mrs. Scott and Mrs. Parker managed to force their way to me to offer hugs and words of comfort. By that time I was in cuffs and it felt really good to have their strong arms around me. After we were separated, scores of questions began to clamor for attention in my mind: How would I break the news to Daniel? Who would pay for an appeal? Would I be locked up there or in Parchman? Before they took me back to a cell, however, I had the presence of mind to secure some matches.

A few hours later I was deliriously happy to be out of jail and back at the SNCC office. The lawyers explained that they had persuaded the judge to suspend the jail term by offering him an irresistible amount of money as a "fine." They said that since I would be on probation and the original sentence could be reinstated at any time, I should leave Mississippi as soon as possible. Haste was necessary, the older of the two lawyers said, because the police had lost a lot of face in front of the black community and they were angry as hell when they learned that I was getting out.

"The judge also lost face," Tilmon said. "People were laughing at him for lighting your cigarettes. But by the time he realized it, it was too late to stop since that would be an admission that you were treating him like a servant."

"He's right," the older lawyer said. "Everyone saw that it was a frame-up. If the judge hadn't taken the money, it's very doubtful you would have come out of jail alive."

His words briefly aroused a sleeping childhood fear. I called Daniel to let him know I was free at last and would be coming home soon. Before we had finished talking, Tilmon asked to speak with Daniel. The first words out of Tilmon's mouth were "You better come get her before she gets us all killed." He said it affectionately, however, and he chuckled afterward, as did everyone in the room. But it was clear that he wasn't kidding about the fact that I had to leave Mississippi.

Chapter Twelve

Home and Away

The bus trip back from Mississippi was not eventful, except for the difficulty of changing buses with luggage and a fire engine big enough for Danny to ride around in. But, happily back in our home a few blocks from the district line in Chevy Chase, Maryland, I found that I was having difficulty shedding the reflexive mistrust I had felt down south for whites I didn't know. I sometimes showed the kind of symptoms associated with paranoia, looking frequently into the rearview mirror when I drove and abruptly changing directions if a car, or especially a pickup truck, seemed to be following me. It sounds counterintuitive, but the best cure for fear of racialists seemed to be immediate involvement in civil rights activities in DC.

While I had been away, Daniel had been involved in a campaign to overcome racially discriminatory practices by Washington's hotels, a major employer in a city with almost no industry except government and tourism. With insider information obtained from a member of the leading hotel employees' union, CORE had initiated negotiations on behalf of a civil rights group that included, in addition to Daniel and Reggie Webb from CORE, attorneys Frank Hollis and Ed Hailes of the NAACP, Rev. Walter Fauntroy from SCLC, and Urban League Director Sterling Tucker, all of whom were friends and visitors to our home. The rather complicated negotiations had included demands that the hotel association not only abolish all racial discrimination but also take affirmative action to recruit minority employees, such as by advertising openings in the *Afro-American* newspapers as well as indicating in white-press want ads that the employer practiced equal opportunity. There was even a demand that the hotel association fund scholarships at the famed Cornell University School of Hotel Administration, as well as at a DC school for hotel work. By design, the rights groups broke off negotiations just before Christmas, citing the persistence of segregated eating facilities for employees of some hotels. "I cry shame on you!" Webb had said as they rose to leave.

A few weeks later we began picketing major hotels, some of which were in the last stages of preparations for President Johnson's inaugural balls. Freezing rain was falling as Daniel and I walked with picket signs up and down the street in front of a large hotel on Inauguration Day eve, occasionally catching a barbed remark in a Texas accent from one of the expensively-dressed guests entering or departing. Each such remark incited grumbling along the line about whether we should be there on this occasion. Having just worked hard to get votes for Johnson in Mississippi, I too felt conflicted, as well as cold and wet, and was not at all pleased when Daniel abandoned me after a messenger arrived to summon him to a meeting with the hotel association. He hadn't returned when the rest of us finally decided we'd had enough misery for one night, and he hadn't returned home when I went to bed after midnight.

Around 2 a.m., Daniel arrived with Frank Hollis and Reggie Webb, the three of them looking as if they had just witnessed a miracle. And to hear them tell it as they broke out the booze, they had. The meeting they had just come from had been convened by one of LBJ's White House troubleshooters, who had said at the outset that he was there at the personal direction of the president of the United States. He then directed both sides to consider each separate demand and proceeded to swat down the hotel association's objections to each one. When he finished, the rights coalition had a signed agreement that gave us virtually everything we had asked for, including scholarships at a hotel management school in DC. Pointing a bony finger at the ceiling and beaming like a biblical prophet, Frank Hollis declared it "the most comprehensive affirmative action agreement ever negotiated." Since he was an attorney in the Office of the US Solicitor General, the rest of us readily agreed, although I wanted to add that it wouldn't have happened if a few foot-soldiers hadn't slogged for hours in the freezing rain.

Despite the recuperative power of the agreement, my faith in white humanity began to ebb once again when our suburban neighbors, even those who were usually friendly, suddenly began to behave strangely. They had not appeared to be alarmed when they learned that, as members of CORE, we were challenging various forms of racial discrimination in the Washington area. From babysitters and in the normal course of events, they must have noticed or heard about our activities, especially since we were not secret about what we were doing or where we stood on civil rights issues. Even after we learned that there were no African American families living in the area, we tended to dismiss that suburban demographic as a relic of the past. After all, the neighborhood had remained calm when Thelton Henderson moved in with us and several whites had been overtly friendly to him, one dropping by to chat much more frequently than we wished. In addition, there had been no complaints that we were aware of about the frequency of visiting African American friends and interracial partying. By 1965 there was even an organization, the Suburban Maryland Fair Housing Association, to assist the first black families to move into the area. We had attended a meeting of that group on our block and been favorably impressed, although we laughed afterward at the chairwoman's advice that if you tell people their new neighbor "is a PhD from MIT, their anxieties will melt away." We understood that the anxieties she mentioned were concerns about whether the value of suburban homes would continue to rise like French soufflé if blacks were able to follow white flight from inner cities. But from the pleasant smiles on the faces of the people at the meeting, we gathered that they were satisfied that their nest eggs were secure.

Not long after that meeting, our next-door neighbors, close friends who had the same landlord as we did and had arranged for us to rent our house, moved away. We had lived there three years and hadn't previously met the elderly couple who owned the two houses, but when we offered to find a replacement tenant, they were very grateful. In answer to our question, they said it didn't matter what color the tenants were as long as they were responsible. We put the word out through CORE and SNCC and soon learned of an interested African American couple and invited them to come over to take a look at the house. They did, but over drinks on our porch afterward, they told us they were looking for something a bit nicer. We learned that they were both PhDs and that he had been hired as an assistant superintendent of county schools and she as an engineer at the Navy's famous boat-design facility a few miles from us on the Potomac. They laughed appreciatively when we told them about the Fair Housing chairwoman's remark about the magical power of a PhD.

About a week later, the wife called to thank us for showing them the house, for our hospitality, and for letting them know about the Fair Housing Association, which she said was now helping them. She said she had told the helpful people in the Association that the Ingrams were also helping them find a home.

"What's a Nigger lover?"

That's the question four-year-old Danny asked me rather breathlessly, coming inside a few days later. Startled, but not wanting to show it, I asked him why he was asking. He said that the other children had told him that they couldn't play with him "because my mommy and daddy are Nigger-lovers." For the next several weeks we were subjected to many remarkably inventive efforts to frighten and harass us into fleeing. Some of the events were so surprising and appalling that we were amazed that they were happening in an affluent community chock-full of high government officials, office holders, professionals, and senior managers of every type of benevolent or public interest organization. Even our babysitters were threatened with harm for taking care of our son. Twice we returned home to find police and a terrified sitter. One Sunday morning, while we were walking with Sondra Dodson, a beautiful African American friend who had come to tell us she had decided to marry Bill Raspberry, the *Washington Post*'s lone black reporter, a police car came racing toward us, screeching to a stop inches away, then sitting there racing its engine until we walked away. We learned, because a friendly neighbor told us, that our tormentors had formed a syndicate to buy our rented house.

Fortunately I was at home and able to fend off a posse from the Society for the Prevention of Cruelty to Animals, which had come to impound Orfeo, our thoroughly pampered standard poodle, in response to reports that we were cruelly abusing him. One of the most upsetting events occurred each day when the Good Humor truck arrived and neighborhood mothers would rush out of their homes and make a big show of buying treats for all the kids, conspicuously excepting Danny. Still we held our ground until an anonymous caller said that it was clear to them (whoever they were) that we were not sufficiently moved by what they had done so far ad therefore they had decided to "go after" our son. Soon after the call, a car drove across our lawn toward Danny. I reached him first, snatched him up, and left that home within an hour, never to return.

I suppose that I shouldn't have been surprised to learn that affluent northern suburbanites could be as vicious as southern Klansmen. We later found out what we should have guessed: the people who chased us back into the District of Columbia had infiltrated the Fair Housing Association to prevent it from helping African Americans move into their neighborhoods. Viewing us as "block-busters" who would bring down home values, the infiltrators were prepared to do whatever it took to protect their golden eggs.

I also should not have been surprised by the news from Moss Point about the deranged black policeman who had been hired by white officials after the black community, which was larger there than the white community, demanded that the force be integrated. I felt like crying when Mrs. Scott wrote that he had beaten his own son to death with his billy club. Tears would have been scalding, however, because I was instantly angry as well as sad. I also saw a connection between the vicious behavior of the whites in Montgomery County who pretended that they welcomed integration and the officials in Moss Point who had pretend to accede to the black community's wishes for a black cop. Although I didn't realize it at the time, the damage done by Moss Point's official cynicism left an emotional scar that turned scarlet twenty years later when Clarence Thomas was appointed to the Supreme Court.

Regardless, instead of feeling like refugees, we were happy to be in DC. When we moved, it was into a charming house on a one-block street down the hill from the Capitol in a section known then as Southeast and now as Capitol Hill. There was no cause to be fearful since our landlord and most of our neighbors were African Americans and none of the whites seemed to be uptight about house prices. And it was a great location, within easy walking distance of the Library of Congress, where world-class chamber music was performed on Stradivarius instruments and the cost of a ticket was twenty-five cents. The Folger Shakespeare Library, a bit farther on, performed Shakespeare plays in a small theater that resembled the ancient Globe. The magnificent National Gallery and Freer Gallery were not much farther, with the beautiful Botanic Garden even closer. Potomac River seafood restaurants with jazz bands—one an all-female group like the one depicted in Some Like it Hot—were also near, as was the floating Maine Avenue Fish Market where I once impulsively rushed between two burly men who were trying to carve up one another with their fish-filleting knives. They were so stunned to have me at blade-point that they stopped fighting, disappointing a circle of onlookers and leaving both Daniel and me pale and shaken. Closer than the fish market was DC's finest theater, Arena Stage, and closer than that in the opposite direction was the funky, partly open-air Eastern Market, where all-night workers or partiers could get breakfast and vendors became friends for life.

Neighbors were friendly and often in the street, so sitting on our stoop in the evening to talk, enjoy my fruit daiquiris, and keep an eye out for Danny and other kids who played in a nearby park, we would soon attract company. Someone would bring a six-pack or two; a journalist or two would saunter by craving martinis; Daniel would stack the Garrard record changer with LPs; two stewardesses would sashay over from across the street; and a party would be underway. Fast talk soon gave way to slow dancing, and candlelight or firelight became the preferred illumination. Maybe it wasn't the drumbeats, but after the dancing started, word of the festivities somehow spread to far reaches of the city. Quite likely, the sounds of music and laughter aroused the entrepreneurial esprit of the neighborhood dealer. Although he had the disconcerting trait of yelling on a crowded street to ask if you wanted more pot, those of us who knew that he was a draft dodger, who baffled the FBI by vanishing inside his apartment when they searched it, felt it our patriotic duty to support his idealism as best we could. On one memorable occasion, when a couple of Mississippi activists were visiting and the dining and living rooms were filled with dancers, the vibrations caused the heavy plaster ceiling to come crashing down, knocking Daniel dizzy but not seriously injuring anyone.

Of course partying wasn't our primary pursuit. Most of our energy was still devoted to driving a stake through the heart of segregation and trying to gain home rule if not statehood for the District of Columbia. To this end, numerous plots of various sorts were hatched or promoted, some eventually successful, such as

"Blacks in Broadcasting," an effort to add people of color to TV newscasts, and others as short-lived as "The People's Theater," which only produced one play while I was its titular president. The plaster ceilings notwithstanding, visiting friends from Mississippi stayed with us when they came to DC to press for voting rights or to seek relief from such punitive actions as the state's refusal to participate in federal food distribution to offset crop failures. On one occasion, our house was used for a meeting to iron out differences between Bayard Rustin and SNCC leaders. I don't remember the issues at hand, but I remember Rustin's response to the question, "Why are you speaking in DC at a rally for Russian Jews who want to emigrate to Israel?" He said that there is an old Hebrew saying that translates to "I am not a Jew because I go to Temple or obey the commandments or observe the holy days and rituals or pray and give thanks. I am a Jew because I believe in the individual dignity of all men."

"That belief is anathema to tyrants," Rustin said, "and it's my belief also."

While he was in our house, Rustin saw the painting he had given to Ed Brown who had given it to me for helping him read *Das Kapital* in its original language. Rustin already knew that I was a Jew who had experienced the firestorm bombing of Hamburg, because his hands had been one of the pairs that calmed me during my déjà vu misery when fireworks exploded over the Atlantic City boardwalk. "I understand that you went to Mississippi after the convention," he said, putting his palms together in front of his beautiful smile. "I'm glad the painting is with you."

The Free DC Movement, a concerted effort to bring home rule to the District of Columbia, grew out of a series of rare political and other events not long after LBJ's inauguration. Carl Stokes, who would later become the first elected black mayor of a major US city, Cleveland, was unable to speak at a CORE conference in DC because our airport was shut down by a severe late-winter snowstorm. As an alternative event, Daniel proposed that we picket the annual banquet of the Greater Washington Board of Trade, a network of business and nonprofit leaders, which had no black members and had recently published ads in newspapers across the country saying that business and professional leaders in DC unanimously opposed home rule. When we reached the banquet hotel—one of the hotels that had hosted an inaugural ball—a dozen demonstrators went inside to hand out home-rule leaflets while the rest picketed outside in the blizzard. Hundreds of guests in formal attire sat at scores of tables for six or eight, in front of and slightly beneath a long head table at which more than thirty members of Congress were guests of honor. Almost all the diners were men and some began to call out to us, using standard racial epithets featuring the N-word. As the number and volume of epithets swelled, a CORE member loudly shouted back, "Is this America?" The response was a negative roar loud enough to rattle the chandeliers. Hotel security personnel rushed to lock all entrances to the room, causing another CORE member to shout "Freedom!" and the rest of us to respond "Now!"

After the third "Now!" there was a sound like an avalanche of boulders as scores of banquet tables were knocked over and hundreds of enraged tradesmen charged us, many of them wielding bottles and at least one with a pistol. From across the room I saw Daniel go down and I may have screamed as I thought he might get trampled to death, but he popped up quickly. Demonstrators who had retreated to the doors were slammed against them and one began to emit bloodcurdling screams. I recognized the screamer as CORE Chairwoman Rowena Rand, a tough-as-steel veteran of the Freedom Rides. She wasn't hurt; she was using her lungs to quiet our berserk assailants. Near Daniel, the man with the gun had it pressed against the temple of a demonstrator who had somehow managed to grab the gunman's balls. Seeing this, Daniel began to yell, "Help! Murder! Call the police! There's a madman with a gun threatening to kill us!" This helped to calm the assailants, and when two cops arrived, Daniel pressed the gun issue and insisted that we be escorted safely away.

The next morning, Daniel, who had wrenched his back during the fracas, collapsed in serious pain when he tried to shovel snow from our steps. Forced to lie in bed the entire next week because ambulances couldn't get down our unplowed street, he recalled JFK's famous advice—don't get mad, get even! And so we plotted to create a rival trade association that would be racially integrated and promote home rule. We knew that many of the Board of Trade's most influential members, including DC's three major newspapers, didn't want to be publicly identified as supporters of racial exclusion and against voting rights. We even fancied White House support, alternative testimony at Congressional hearings, and newspaper ads debunking the Board of Trade's ads.

Unfortunately, while Daniel was on the phone explaining the project to *Washington Post* reporter Bill Raspberry, we were visited by one of SNCC Chairman Marion Barry's close advisors, a rumpled, middle-aged, white mystery man who squinted and talked out of one side of his mouth because he kept a lit cigarette dangling from the other side. Ed Brown thought he might be either an FBI agent or a Communist plant, but I saw him as typecast for a grade-B gangster movie. Whatever he was, he had Marion Barry's ear and he let us know that he didn't think much of our plan to organize business support for home rule. DC CORE embraced the plan, however, and began preparations to implement it. So when Barry announced a similar-sounding plan, CORE Chairwoman Rowena Rand protested privately that he was plagiarizing. This led to a "trial" before the DC Coalition of Conscience, an informal group of civil rights and church leaders, with SCLC's Rev. Walter Fauntroy serving as chief judge. The unsurprising verdict was that the Free DC Movement would be led by the charismatic Barry, who had earned his spurs in Mississippi and had directed an impressive one-day boycott of DC buses. With great graphics, good press, and the support of luminaries in the Coalition of Conscience, including the bishop who served as dean of the National Cathedral, Barry ringed department stores with pickets demanding financial support for Free DC.

It was instantly clear to us that Barry had badly misunderstood Daniel's theory that if businessmen were persuaded to form an integrated association and challenge the Board of Trade's positions on home rule, they would pick up the costs of organizing and operating such a group. Daniel thought such costs would be trivial as business expenses, but he so hated fund-raising to finance CORE projects that he had cited business financing as a virtue when he outlined the plan to Barry's advisor. However, instead of persuading businessmen to join the fight for home rule, Barry and cohorts were trying to compel them to make friends to contribute money to our cause. Unfortunately for the home-rule movement, the US Attorney for DC soon denounced that tactic as criminal extortion, causing many Free DC supporters to run for cover. The home-rule issue didn't die, however, and Barry's image as its black knight served him and sometimes DC well for the rest of his colorful life.

While DC's aspirations for home rule were simmering, the lid blew off of almost a century of voting rights suppression in the South. Forty-five days after LBJ's inauguration, some six hundred African Americans in Selma, Alabama tried to demonstrate just how fed up they were with white suppression of their right to vote. During the preceding weeks, thousands of their neighbors and their neighbors' children had been arrested, scores had been beaten and abused, and one man, Jimmie Lee Jackson, had been brutally killed. With children in tow, the six hundred began a protest march to the state capital, Montgomery, Alabama, several hundred miles distant. As they were walking across the Edmund Pettus Bridge, leaving Selma, they were attacked by an armed contingent of state troopers who blinded them with tear gas and charged them on foot and on horseback, riding into them and after them, cracking skulls, breaking bones, and spilling blood with heavy truncheons. Within hours, millions of television viewers were first aghast and then incensed as scenes of the onslaught were repeated throughout the day. Demonstrations of support for the victims of "Bloody Sunday" quickly followed, with DC as a focal point for pressure to get federal protection for another voting rights march from Selma to Montgomery. A mega-rally in DC severely tested the ability of area police to keep masses of protesters at a distance from the White House, inside which, unbeknownst to us, LBJ was composing his speech of a lifetime.

When he delivered it to a joint session of Congress eight days after Bloody Sunday, even those of us who wildly applauded our TV sets were left speechless by Johnson's passionate embrace of the civil rights cause. Insisting that our cause should be everyone's cause, he made the strongest possible case for the passage of voting-rights legislation. He then told the nation "it's all of us who must overcome the crippling legacy of bigotry and injustice," triumphantly adding, "and we shall overcome!" And Congress thundered applause at this invocation of the most familiar refrain in the movement's anthem! After recovering our breath, Daniel and I went outside to see if flights of angels were perched upon the Capitol dome. We didn't see any angels, but they must have been there somewhere, because the transformative Voting Rights Act became law five months later.

My mother visited us during this period and participated in some of many demonstrations. She couldn't remain "nonviolent," however, when we encountered a counterdemonstration by members of the American Nazi Party who were uniformed and capped like storm troopers, complete with swastika armbands. Remembering what the real *sturmtruppen* had done to her and her family, she was unable to contain her fury. When one of the American Nazis threw an egg at us, she broke ranks, ran across the street, and began to pummel him. With a little police assistance, I retrieved her and took her home to recuperate. After that, she let me know that she understood why I had gone to Mississippi and might have done the same in my shoes.

Also around this time, Daniel witnessed an event that exemplified the dire consequences of ignored poverty. He was driving up U Street in northwest Washington when a truck directly in front of him struck and killed a small African American boy. After the truck stopped, its left rear tire was squarely on top of the boy's crushed body. Police quickly arrived and prevented Daniel from leaving the scene for almost an hour. A police officer eventually placed a tarpaulin over the boy's shoulders, head, and outstretched arms. This of course did not relieve Daniel's heartbreak. The child was only a few years older than our son, who had been knocked down by a passing car a few months earlier. Danny had appeared to be gravely injured when I lifted him from the gutter and we raced by car to the nearest hospital, but fortunately his injuries were not as serious as they looked. The officers who interviewed Daniel beside the partially covered boy were not as anguished as Daniel, but were more surprised that the youth had ventured into the dense, swiftly moving noon-day traffic on U Street. We had difficulty sleeping that night and greater difficulty with our normal routine the next day when we learned that the child had been rushing home, as he did each school day, to share his school lunch with a younger brother and sister. It was the family's main source of nourishment. Not long after that, Daniel declined a higher-paying job to accept one with DC's War on Poverty.

President Johnson's "We Shall Overcome" speech didn't end the picket line in front of the White House or prevent other mega-rallies demanding federal protection for Selma marchers. After one, Dr. George Wiley, a professor at Syracuse University and an associate director of CORE, conducted a master class on demonstrating. He pointed out that by ignoring "keep off the grass" signs, we might have caused the government to commit the troops which were waiting in troop carriers just outside the city, ready to rush in if the demonstration got out of hand. Having responded with troops to save the grass, Dr. Wiley reasoned, the government would have difficulty denying our demand for federal protection in Selma. To illustrate how we might use our tactical imaginations to gain strategic advantages, Dr. Wiley asked us to picket the Washington

Monument at midnight, which we did. Fairly soon, the monument was surrounded by at least a dozen police cars, which began to drive toward us, slowly tightening a noose. When they were about fifteen yards away, Wiley had us kneel and pray or pretend to pray. The police halted and an official or two got out of a car. Dr. Wiley calmly walked over and told them he was an out-of-town professor giving informal instructions on the origins of our freedoms and was terribly sorry he had alarmed the police. The police turned their cars around and headed back to somewhere, and we walked single file to a major thoroughfare where, hand in outstretched hand, we blocked traffic. We stopped traffic briefly at different places, with a different spokesperson each time promising to end the demonstration. About the fourth or fifth time, however, a police cruiser charged toward us at such a high speed that it was obvious that he would not be able to stop if he tried. We jumped out of his way and scattered, class ended by "the fuzz," which was a favorite name for the police, especially when they looked foolish.

Our antics may have made them sore, however, because the next time I went to the White House picket line, the police almost immediately arrested every one of us. The ridiculous-sounding charge was "discommoding the sidewalk," and it was based on the rather absurd claim that some of us were seen walking with fewer than sixty inches of separation between us. I suppose I was guilty, since I was talking to the person in front of me at the time of the bust. A policeman grabbed me roughly, twisted my arm behind my back, and was attempting to throw me into a paddy wagon when a black policeman separated us and helped me climb in. The latter also gallantly helped me dispose of a joint I had brought to give to a former cohort from Mississippi who had sent me a message that she was on the line. I had thrown a raincoat over a flimsy dress and gone to the line to greet her, but she had already gone and I landed in jail with no ID or money for bail. Fortunately, Earl Tilden, a fellow CORE member who was also arrested, arranged our bail and took me home. A gleaming array of police brass and top prosecutors turned out for the trial, and we were represented by ACLU lawyers eager to challenge the constitutionality of the arrests. I sat beside our lead counsel, local ACLU director Ralph Temple, who was also a friend and CORE colleague. The judge, one of DC's few black jurists, could see that both sides were righteously primed for a doomsday battle, and he soon found a way to reduce the case to an unfortunate misunderstanding. When one of the defendants said she didn't hear the police warn us to keep a proper distance, the judge asked those who hadn't heard a warning to raise their hand. Several did, and the judge dismissed the case, saying there obviously had been no intent to break the law. As Ralph smiled and Daniel winced, I raised my hand and told the judge I had heard the police warn us. The judge banged his gavel and shot me a look I shall never forget. It was benevolent—he clearly understood that I was trying to raise the Constitutional issue—but he was also rock hard, letting me know, "Not in my court you won't!" He then looked from me to the door and back again, allowing the faintest of smiles to crack the rock. Smiling back and getting up to leave, I had the warm feeling of having made a new friend.

Of the several CORE-ACLU actions we engaged in with Ralph Temple, the saddest was a police brutality case that looked for a time like a huge advance and ended in a near-fatal tragedy. In part because police violence had sparked riots in several other cities, the ACLU and CORE wanted to improve police-community relations and public safety by establishing an independent review board in DC to hear complaints and punish serious misconduct. And we got a review board in that case, which grew out of the arrest of two heavily bearded black men who were standing with a young white woman as she waited to catch a cab a few minutes past closing time outside a small DC nightspot. The men were the cabaret's musicians and the woman was its last customer that morning; however, two policemen happened by and arrested the men, who were hit with night sticks and later charged with resisting arrest. The police claimed they had made the arrests because the men looked like the bank robbers on recent "wanted" circulars. At the trial, however, CORE-ACLU attorneys proved there had been no recent circulars or alerts for black bank robbers, with or without beards. CORE immediately demanded independent disciplinary hearings, and in time Daniel and a few others sat in all night in the offices of the DC commissioners and pressed the case when the commissioners arrived the next morning. Days later, hallelujah! An independent review board was announced—possibly DC's first—with a Howard University professor as one of its three members. Some CORE members were so certain that the officers would be fired that they even wanted to recommend clemency for one of them who "seemed like a nice guy." The motion failed, and I attended the historic trial that followed.

We were not terribly surprised that the police summoned a black "witness" to say he had heard and seen the musicians disturbing the peace and resisting the police on the night in question. But we and the police were amazed when the witness arrived with his priest to tell the panel he had been pressured by the police to give such false testimony. The next day I saw no need to return. The police officers had flagrantly solicited perjury to cover up earlier perjury and brutality. Case closed, I thought, but then I got a call from Ralph Temple asking me to rush back because the lawyers for the police had told the judges (and everyone within earshot) that the witness had changed his story because the slender, dark-haired, white woman present yesterday had promised or granted him "unusual sexual favors." I returned to refute their lie, but did not testify. Thankfully, the officers were found guilty; however, they were fined all of a princely sum of twenty-five dollars each. Someone said the hat was being passed at the precinct house to cover the fines, and the smiles on police faces made me think it must be true.

A far greater offense occurred nights later at the rural Virginia home of the woman who had been trying to get a cab when the arrests were made. She was a Quaker and for that reason hadn't wanted to testify at the hearing, but Ralph had persuaded her that her testimony would help discourage future acts of brutality by people who had presumably sworn to protect us. After the trial, and after several phone calls accusing her of having sex with black men, she was alarmed to see several grim men, one with a rope, walking across the grass toward her isolated house. She phoned the sheriff's office and requested help that never came. The men slashed her face and breast and choked her with the rope until she was nearly dead. Recuperating in a hospital, she called the sheriff's office again but was told it could do nothing unless she gave them the names of black men she had slept with.

Able to do little else at the time, Temple used CORE's program on one of DC's most popular radio stations, WOL, a.k.a. Soul Radio, to tell the public the woman's story. Dewey Hughes, the young WOL journalist who helped with CORE's program, also accompanied us to the Board of Trade banquet and taped the assault on protesters. The story he filed about that event was his first to be rebroadcast on national radio networks and helped propel a career that included eventual ownership of the station.

Achieving home rule proved to be more problematic than passing the revolutionary Voting Rights Act. We made another effort, however, when we heard that Martin Luther King, Jr., was considering protesting against racial oppression in northern cities. Since our friend, neighbor, and former CORE leader Norman Hill would be attending the SCLC meeting at which a decision would be made, Daniel and I pumped him full of reasons why DC should be a target and home rule the issue, and asked him to advocate for DC if a decision was made to protest discrimination in the North. When Norm returned to DC, he told us that Bayard Rustin had opened the debate with a brilliant analysis of the differences in the ways northern and southern officials dealt with racial protests, concluding that SCLC's confrontational style might not be effective in the North, where sheriffs and governors smile on camera and break your bones when no one's looking.

We asked Norm what King's response was and were told that King had teared up, opened his arms wide, and said to the entire room, "But God told me to go north!"

Daniel asked Norm what Bayard had replied. Norm shrugged and asked, "What can you say to that?"

After Dr. King bared his soul on the subject, there was no more debate about whether SCLC should invade the North, but only a discussion of which cities should be targeted. At that point, Norm Hill made the case for DC and Dr. King and others agreed, especially Reverend Walter Fauntroy, who was DC's main man in SCLC and SCLC's main man in DC. At the end of the conference, Walter privately thanked Norm for standing up for DC and said he had not known until then that Norm had left New York. Norm told him that he and his wife, Velma Hill, had moved into a house two doors down from the Ingrams and the four of us had spent hours discussing DC's needs and prospects.

In other cities, especially Chicago, King was less welcome than Attila the Hun would be, but in DC he was embraced with open arms. After attending a series of neighborhood meetings during the day, he made a stirring address to thousands of people outside an inner-city church, and then we all marched through the night to Lafayette Square, a park across from the White House, for a spirited home-rule rally. King also spoke there and promised to return to DC and march again and again until Washingtonians could vote with their hands and not just their feet. President Johnson apparently got the message. In the months that followed, he pressed Congress for home-rule legislation, and about a year later we got an appointed mayor and city council, and the right to elect our school board. Five years later, in 1973, we were allowed to elect the mayor and city council, but Congress retained veto powers and denied us many of the fundamental rights normally exercised by other cities. Today, the citizens of the "capital of the free world" are allowed to elect a spokesperson to make our wishes known to Congress, but he or she is not allowed to vote, and presidents from both parties have used DC license plates protesting our "taxation without representation." The first time Washingtonians were able to vote for a president was 1964.

Daniel and I continued to be activists throughout the turbulent and frequently tragic sixties. When Martin Luther King, Jr., was assassinated on April 4, 1968, one year to the day after his condemnation of the Vietnam War, Daniel was the information director for the United Planning Organization (UPO), the antipoverty agency for the Washington area. He spent most of that night in the apartment of UPO's director, Wiley Branton, an outstanding black civil rights attorney who had posed as a white attorney to southern sheriffs to inveigle the release of rights workers jailed on trumped-up charges. Branton had also served in the Justice Department under Presidents Kennedy and Johnson and had come to know and love Dr. King in Atlanta while heading a voter-registration program that had enabled 600,000 black southerners to vote. When Dr. King received the Nobel Prize, he asked Branton to distribute half the prize money to civil rights groups other than SCLC, which received the other half. King did this to acknowledge publicly that the civil rights movement was a collaborative effort.

Daniel's job on the night of King's assassination was to field media requests for statements from Branton who, as the head of a community-action agency, with offices, organizers, and affiliated citizen groups in low-income areas throughout the city, was expected to encourage African Americans to grieve in peace and not let their anger become violent. Instead, Branton asked Daniel to tell the media he was not available. A true-blue believer in nonviolence and the rule of law, who would later be dean of Howard Law School,

Branton told Daniel that the nation "must understand that there are some things we will not accept, otherwise no black leader's life will be safe." Throughout the burning and the military occupation of DC that followed, Daniel went to work every day in a so-called "riot zone." The only person in a seven-story office building, he coordinated deliveries of food, water, medicine, and other emergency services to low-income neighborhoods experiencing unprecedented fires and smoke from torched businesses and an invasion by armed troops arrayed for battle. Fortunately, unlike troops summoned to several other cities, those in DC did not shoot to kill. I attributed that to the civilized direction of Cyrus Vance, who was appointed by LBJ to oversee martial law in DC and who later was President Carter's Secretary of State. Years later, I also gave posthumous credit to DC Mayor Walter Washington when I learned that FBI Director J. Edgar Hoover had told him to order DC police to shoot looters and Washington had refused, saying that goods in stores could be replaced, but not human lives.

When Richard Nixon succeeded to the Oval Office, he assigned three political operatives to dismantle the national War on Poverty while he and Henry Kissinger defoliated and depopulated Vietnam and Cambodia. Daniel and lots of others did their best to restrain anti-antipoverty warrior-in-chief Donald Rumsfeld; his top aide, Frank Carlucci; and their sidekick, Dick Cheney, who considered his gig more important than military service. At one point Daniel arranged for syndicated columnist Jack Anderson to reveal their "top secret" plans to slash or eliminate funding for preschool, daycare, employment, health, education, savings, and other programs. Daniel and one of his colleagues, Calvin Rolark, also held a press conference with more than a thousand concerned citizens as invited guests outside the national headquarters of the Office of Economic Opportunity (OEO), which administered the antipoverty war. After learning the scope of budget cuts, hundreds of angry women from the National Welfare Rights Organization (created by Dr.

George Wiley) stormed the headquarters, confronting Carlucci and pounding on Rumsfeld's locked door, shouting, "Come out of there, you motherfucker, and face reality!"

For bravely battling the poor and powerless, each member of Nixon's dynamic trio was later rewarded by being appointed secretary of defense, with control over the world's largest budget and its most powerful armed forces. Rumsfeld became the only man to serve twice as armaments czar, while Carlucci chaired an investment fund that apparently prospered by picking winners in the defense contracting industry. Daniel went on to work for nonprofits such as the Minority Contractors Assistance Project and the Cooperative Assistance Fund, trying to promote economic development in low-income communities. Although he believes that anyone who tries to reduce poverty should expect to have his heart broken and his ass kicked, he loved his work and he and his colleagues occasionally enjoyed modest success.

And then one day Daniel was asked by an aide to Maryland Congressman Parren Mitchell how black construction workers might benefit from legislation then in the pipeline to reduce unemployment by spending billions of dollars on public works projects. At the time, few white contractors had more than a token number of minority workers, and less than a handful of minority contractors ever landed government contracts. Daniel and his boss at the Minority Contractors Assistance Project, Dickie Carter, believed their experience suggested a workable approach. Daniel told the aide that a current subway project in Mitchell's Baltimore district had demonstrated that the only way to include minority workers was to require that ten percent of the work go to minority contractors. He invited the aide to check out the idea with people in the subway's contracts division. Ten days later, while the press was out to lunch, Congressman Mitchell managed to insert such a requirement in the bill, and black Republican Senator Ed Brooke later inserted the same language in the Senate version of the bill.

Six breathless weeks later, on May 23, 1977, a bill with the proviso was signed into law by President Jimmy Carter.

Daniel broke the story of the act's minority contracting requirement in the *New York Times* through one of its few black reporters, Ernie Holzendorf, and a volcano of white-hot protest erupted. The *Wall Street Journal* cried foul; *Fortune* magazine called the law the most odiferous legislation ever to rise from the banks of the Potomac; a *60 Minutes* reporter asked TV viewers if they would like to ride in an elevator that had been installed by a minority contractor; and some fifty lawsuits were filed in federal courts throughout the United States, many of them backed by a national construction industry task force created to fight the law.

Despite such rabid opposition, minority contractors fulfilled contracts that billed hundreds of millions of dollars and provided jobs for thousands of minority workers. When the fifty lawsuits reached the Supreme Court, Daniel advised researchers for the Justice Department attorneys who defended the law, and he filed an amicus curiae (friend of the court) brief on behalf of minority contractors. Another surprise: we won, with a strong opinion from Wiley Branton's friend and former colleague, Justice Thurgood Marshall.

Dickie Carter and Daniel also lobbied the DC government to take similar measures to increase the amount of public work performed by minority businesses and employees. Despite the opposition of white business groups that were used to getting ninety-seven percent of the contracts let by the city, such measures were put in place after Marion Barry became mayor. Passage of the federal law spurred a number of other cities and states to take similar steps to include minority-owned businesses when contracting for public works and services.

Dismay over the dismantling of the War on Poverty was at least partially offset by the gathering strength of the fight to end the war in Southeast Asia. It was heartening to participate in the epic waves of protest that caused the White House to erect barricades of empty buses and the Pentagon to deploy thousands of troops to confront an army of children armed with flowers. Of course it was also discouraging after the May Day demonstrations in 1971 to hear the lions of the press and their influential guests at the White House correspondents' banquet roar their approval for the DC police chief who had illegally arrested thousands of us. The pretext for the largest mass arrests in US history was that some of the protesters had threatened to block rush-hour traffic flowing past the Capitol. I'm glad that Nixon, who was exercising remote control from his home in California, didn't arrange to have tanks handy to clear the intersections. I and more than a thousand other lawful peaceniks listening to antiwar speeches were herded from Capitol Hill to Robert F. Kennedy stadium at least a mile away, where we were confined in an outdoor fenced-off compound that lacked basic facilities, such as water and toilets. Almost all of us were later released without charges—the courts and jails were so overcome they couldn't process us—and we were glad we hadn't been treated like black Congressman Ron Dellums, who was clubbed after identifying himself to a cop who said he didn't "give a fuck" who Dellums was. Neither Daniel, who had a cold, nor I were at the broadcast media's banquet, but Daniel's boss and friend Dickie Carter attended as the guest of Hal Walker, CBS's first black correspondent, and believes that he and Hal were the only ones there who didn't join in the standing ovation for the police chief whose force broke the law thousands of times in three days.

Martin Puryear, having completed a fellowship at the Royal Swedish Academy of Art in Stockholm, came home to DC from Yale's Graduate School of Arts in New Haven to participate in several antiwar protests. Rendezvousing at our house on Capitol Hill before a march, Martin invariably introduced us to fellow students as the people who had saved his life by talking him into joining the Peace Corps rather that entering the Army Officer Candidate School. Unfortunately, another dear friend, Joe Henriques, a Navy fighter pilot who had wanted to become the first black astronaut, didn't agree until it was too late that the human suffering caused by the Vietnam War made it a catastrophe rather than a cause worth dying for. After demonstrating exceptional bravery during a number of missions, he was killed, leaving his lovely wife without a husband and his three beautiful children without a father.

Congresswoman Shirley Chisholm of Brooklyn, New York, became the first black woman to serve in the US House of Representatives by defeating CORE founder and civil rights hero James Farmer in 1968. Naturally I had rooted for Farmer, the pacifist Freedom Rider who had paid scads of dues with imprisonment, courage, and years of hard labor for the principles he championed and I shared. But I soon came to respect the voters' choice. Representative Chisholm was a savvy legislator with a staff of black and white women, who tackled practical problems for working families, especially problems exacerbated by poverty and racial and gender inequality. With Congresswoman Bella Abzug, for example, she initiated legislation for national child-care services, which was watered down but passed by the House and the Senate, only to be vetoed by President Nixon. So in 1972 when she launched a serious run for the democratic presidential nomination, I went to Florida to work in her campaign. We didn't expect to win the nomination, but she was able to use her candidacy as a bully pulpit to call for an end to the carnage in Southeast Asia, where an outsized number of black draftees were in the line of fire.

When Shirley Chisholm first started attacking the Vietnam War, there were very few high-level elected or appointed officials with the courage to do so. One other feisty black woman, however, caused a national hissy fit and got Daniel in hot water with her comments about the war. Actress Eartha Kitt had been invited from Los Angeles to DC by the first lady, Lady Bird Johnson, to attend a luncheon conference on the problems of American youths. Before the luncheon, Kitt let Daniel know she would be available for a press conference that afternoon to stimulate support for an antipoverty program for black youths that was in danger of being scrapped. Daniel hastily arranged for a press conference in the offices of Chicago Congressman Roman Pucinski, who had supported the program earlier at Kitt's behest and was eager to get together with her again. But not long after the lunch hour, the congressman's office called to say that Pucinski was not available for the rest of the day. So Daniel even more hastily steered the press to the office of his boss, UPO Director Wiley Branton. Both Wiley and Daniel were impressed when national and local reporters showed up with truckloads of television equipment, but were taken aback when a TV interviewer asked the first question:

"Miss Kitt, did you go to the White House today with the deliberate intention of insulting the president's wife?"

Before she could answer, Branton rose from his seat beside her and excused himself from the room, explaining, "Obviously, you and Miss Kitt have things to discuss that I know nothing about." The next day everyone who read a newspaper or watched TV knew that Eartha had told Lady Bird that if she wanted to help American youth she should get her husband to stop sending them to Vietnam. Although the president was furious, Branton accepted Daniel's explanation that there was no way he could have known in advance about Kitt's statement, which might have seriously injured their antipoverty efforts if she had repeated them on camera while seated beside Branton. As Kitt later acknowledged, her comment almost wrecked her career because it was interpreted by many as rude and unpatriotic. To her credit, she never recanted.

From its first day, Daniel and I participated in what became the longest and arguably the most successful civil rights protest in America—and Americans were not its direct beneficiaries. That protest against apartheid in South Africa began with picketing and arrests at the nation's Washington embassy in late November of 1984. Those arrested were the founding leaders of the Free South Africa Movement (FSAM); Dr. Randall Robinson, founder of TransAfrica;

Commissioner Mary Frances Berry of the US Commission on Civil Rights; and Walter Fauntroy, who had become DC's elected but nonvoting representative in Congress. Because there were so few demonstrators, I didn't miss a day of picketing during the first weeks, letting such things as the opening exhibition of my fiber art at a local gallery go unattended.

In fairly short order, however, the demonstration gained traction as members of the Congressional Black Caucus and other congressmen and civil rights leaders joined the cause, and DC mayor Marion Barry made it as easy as it was commendable to get arrested and released. Celebrities, politicians, and thousands of decent people viewed such an arrest record as a badge of honor. Labor and student groups organized protests and demanded that unions and universities withdraw funds invested in South Africa. Despite strenuous opposition from the Reagan White House, Congress passed legislation calling for sanctions against the apartheid government, and when Reagan vetoed it, Congress gave him a legislative black eye by overriding his veto. In time, Nelson Mandela and other prisoners were released and South Africa became an inclusive republic.

Not all our protests worked out well, however. In 1980, seven years after Daniel and I bought a DC house near the Potomac River (for four thousand dollars down), our neighbor, Michael Halberstam, the brother of a favorite author and Vietnam war correspondent and critic, David Halberstam, was shot and killed by a burglar from Virginia. Having seen protests shorten a shooting war abroad, I decided to try to get something started that might reduce the appalling gun violence at home. I organized a protest of mothers with small children, some babies in prams and toddlers in strollers and some old enough to walk, outside National Rifle Association (NRA) offices in the area. We thought we had won the day when an armed NRA official threatened on camera "to blow your fucking heads off." I told everyone to go home and watch the NRA shoot itself in the foot on TV news. Daniel rented a television set and bought champagne so we could watch and celebrate victory at the same time. But TV stations refused to show that footage. In fact, there was a complete press blackout of the event, and I realized that the NRA could do whatever it pleased, even run guns to killers, and not be called to account by the media.

One of our last hurrahs before moving to Italy was a campaign to repeal the Kennedy Center's decision to stop selling "standing room" tickets at opera and ballet performances. From its first opening night, the highly subsidized center had made standing room available at prices low-income aficionados might afford. During the national bicentennial in 1976, cultural junkies stood in line all night to see and hear the great opera and ballet companies and orchestras of the world that had come to DC to help America celebrate. But several years later, after the Reagan administration inherited the power to appoint center trustees and cut or swell government subsidies, standing room was suddenly abolished at the center an hour before a performance of *Der Rosenkavalier* by the Metropolitan Opera Company from New York, which was blamed for the cancellation. Daniel quickly formed a committee to meet with the top Met executive present, who turned out to be the man who had been Daniel's stage director twenty years earlier. Asked if the Met had discontinued standing room in DC, Assistant Executive Director Stanley Levine replied, "Heavens no! We no longer have a say in such matters. These days, we are packaged and sold like soap flakes!"

We saw the opera that night but there was no standing room for weeks during which we picketed and petitioned to no avail, even though almost all members of the National Symphony Orchestra and the New York Philharmonic signed our petition. Our breakthrough came when Senator Ted Kennedy sent a letter of support and also contacted Kennedy Center Director Roger Stevens, who sent word that he was willing to meet with us. We brought a negotiating committee composed of people who did useful work for little or no money—a nurse, a music student, an artist, an emergency-room attendant, a teacher, a composer, a child-care giver, etc. After a few sometimes stormy meetings, we learned that certain new patrons (who wore furs, suntans, and lots of jewelry) objected to walking past us as they swanned toward expensive seats (likely purchased by military-industrial lobbyists). In response we quoted JFK's golden words on the center's walls, to the effect that the nation's performance arts should be for all the people. Stevens agreed and executed a contract which provided "in perpetuity" forty standing room places at half the price of the cheapest seat for the performance. When we received our copy of the contract, Daniel reminded me that my first American protest had been to save Carnegie Hall.

* * *

When I reflect on the causes I embraced and protests I participated in, I always credit my father for teaching me to stand up to injustice. Of course he instructed me to do that, but I have never been one to do as I am told, so it was his example that shaped my convictions and behavior. As a young child I took it for granted that he would care for me and our family, but even then I knew that he was special. He was not a Jew, but he defied the Nazis by staying with his Jewish wife and family, and he was ostracized, beaten nearly to death, and had his business confiscated for helping us. Forced into the *Luftwaffe* (German air force) and stationed in Belgium, he risked his life and was imprisoned for months by the Gestapo for helping Belgian Jews. Defiance of evil must have been in his and therefore my DNA, because his six brothers also resisted Nazism, and one killed himself to avoid giving information while he was being interrogated by the SS for collaborating with the French underground.

Father didn't stop fighting fascists and helping others escape tyranny when the war ended. I learned from my stepmother after his death that he had made several trips into East Germany to smuggle her relatives and others out of that oppressive regime. When he visited us in Washington in 1972, his suitcase was stuffed with documents relating to his efforts to expose Nazis who had returned to public offices. In this endeavor, he had me recount into a tape recorder some of my postwar experiences in Hamburg with anti-Semitic school officials and others. He loved Washington's museums and galleries and endeared himself to our friends by his vivacious personality and by stopping to chat with every beggar or homeless person he encountered. The following year he died as a result of kidney problems dating back to his beating by Nazi storm troopers.

Years after my mother had divorced him and moved to America, Father pressed a claim in her behalf seeking reparations for property taken from her family by the Nazis. In that pursuit, he wrote to me in DC to try to document the purchase of a Shakespeare First Folio by my mother's father when he was living in New York at the turn of the century. The First Folio had been confiscated by the Nazis, and my father wanted to include this loss in my mother's claim. The sale had been negotiated by a New York publisher at a time when there were only two First Folios in America, but the publisher refused to identify my grandfather as the buyer, asserting that the buyer had requested anonymity. After researching the matter, the chief curator of First Folios at the Folger Shakespeare Library in Washington volunteered to go to Germany and testify that my grandfather had been the purchaser. The German government, however, insisted that my mother return to testify in person. She told her daughters that she didn't want to return, but would if we insisted. Of course we didn't.

I never stopped wondering what became of that folio, however, and hoping that its presence might suddenly become known with its provenance intact. The curator thought that it still existed, possibly in Great Britain, and that its cover and condition put it in a top category of surviving folios. He took Daniel and me into the walk-in safe or repository where the Folger collection is maintained for posterity, and even let me touch and examine some of the fabulously bound folios. They were not bound when they were printed, he explained, so each binding, if there is one, is different, and the history of a folio through the ages is often the subject of a book. Of course I often think about my grandparents, Rosa Wolff and Siegfried Singer, and am thrilled to recall that they purchased and I handled a Shakespeare First Folio.

It's fair to say, though sometimes disputed, that the civil rights movement in the sixties produced monumental advances for minorities and plowed the ground for the antiwar, feminist, environmental, and gay rights movements that followed. Two remarkable southerners—polar opposites, antagonists, and ultimately collaborators—are now given most of the credit for those advances, and it is probably true that little would have been achieved without the extraordinary talents and timely presence of both Martin Luther King, Jr., and Lyndon Baines Johnson. It's also likely that the two men would have ended up looking more like Don Quixote and Sancho Panza and less like superheroes, if they had they not been impelled as well as followed by a movement of thousands of courageous men and women and sometimes children. Carrying the banners of several very different organizations, these protesters endured the outrages of racial supremacists and the apathy and antipathy of most Americans. For me, as a survivor of war and genocide, it was a transforming experience to play a very small part in a peaceful revolution by the meek against the powerful. I was not one, but there were hundreds of genuine heroes who risked their lives over and over again, inspiring and sometimes shaming the rest of us. Many were and remain unknown, even to one another. And as we overcame, I overcame. I shed the fear and rage that goes with being a victim, and gained the confidence and deep satisfaction that comes from defeating prejudice by subtle means.

The violence that accompanied some of the protests was often blamed on rights activists. We were called outside agitators, provocateurs, and bullies of gentle southern folk who, Nobel literary laureate William Faulkner insisted, wanted to proceed at their own pace to admit impediment to "the Southern way of life." But the violence was not our doing; we didn't fight back even to defend ourselves from injury. If blood was shed, it was the blood of blacks and the whites who stood with them.

As for the urban riots of that period, suburbanites probably should not be expected to understand why ghetto dwellers could become so enraged that they would torch their own neighborhood in response to one more instance of police abuse on a hot day. It was easier for me to understand an uprising by people systematically marginalized and confined to a ghetto than it was to explain acceptance of such conditions. I also understood the instinct to defend family and tribe and to strike back at those who attacked them; however, having seen what a technologically advanced but morally backward majority can do to a minority group, I firmly believed that nonviolent concerted action was the only sane tactic available in the US. Unfortunately, too many others saw things differently.

Success took some of the steam out of the movement as many activists, like Daniel, tried to put meat on the bones of newly-won rights by enlisting in the War on Poverty. But prolonged failure to secure basic needs was much more destabilizing. Good schools, housing, and job opportunities remained out of reach for all but a few African Americans. Arrests, imprisonments, and the use of deadly force were increasingly viewed as necessary to constrain those whom politicians dismissed as beyond redemption. Excesses by movement leaders vying for "relevance" and media attention greatly accelerated the decline. As stimulating as it had been to hear Stokely Carmichael declare "black is beautiful," it was depressing when this nonviolent assailant of Jim Crow began to talk up separatism and armed struggle. After a firebrand speech at Howard University in which he called LBJ a "honky," he shocked those around him by embracing me, lifting me up, and swinging me around as if he genuinely missed the days when blacks and whites in SNCC were brothers and sisters. Ed Brown's younger brother, Rap, who had partied at our house, was even more reckless in speaking about weapons and violence after he succeeded Carmichael as SNCC chairman, which he said was "as American as cherry pie." As early as 1966, CORE's new leader, Floyd McKissick, said that CORE protesters would begin to defend themselves; and SNCC, in 1969, dropped "Nonviolent" from its name. Overheated rhetoric, coupled with the actual violence of a few extremists, made it easier for law enforcement agencies to use unlawful tactics, including assassination, to disrupt, discredit, and manipulate rights groups. Fred Hampton, a charismatic Black Panther in Chicago, was shot forty-four times in his bed during one of several deadly police raids orchestrated by the FBI in various cities. These were extreme examples of an illicit campaign against rights groups that had been going on for several years under the FBI code name COINTELPRO (an acronym for COunter INTELligence PROgram). The specter of "black power" also provided the cover for segregationists to reinvent themselves as "conservatives" and work to keep schools, churches, and neighborhoods black, white, and unequal.

When Ronald Reagan rode into Washington wearing cowboy boots and a smile that Arthur Miller's Willy Loman would have killed for, he came via the "southern strategy," which posited that the road to the White House ran through the South, where electoral votes could be gathered in bunches by pandering to racial prejudice. In a theatrical enactment of that theory, Reagan launched his campaign in the Mississippi community where CORE workers James Chaney, Michael Schwerner, and Andrew Goodman had been murdered. There, instead of honoring the martyrs, he proclaimed his belief in "states' rights" to an audience and region that interpreted that position as opposition to federally enforced integration. To make sure his message was understood, Reagan followed up with a pilgrimage to Bob Jones University, a Christian university in South Carolina where racial separation was an article of faith. In speeches to northern audiences he, audiences, he depicted recipients of public assistance as "welfare queens" who collected their checks in Cadillacs. One Reagan advertisement imagined a "big buck" buying steaks with food stamps while a working man was forced to feed his family hamburgers. After greatly increasing the Pentagon's already recently increased budget, Reagan picked one of the coldest nights in years to demonstrate his distaste for non-military spending by having the heat turned off in public buildings in downtown DC. He also demonstrated his fiscal conservatism by turning off a light in the White House portico facing Pennsylvania Avenue. According to an article in the *Washington Post*, on the morning after the heat was turned off, clean-up crews collected the frozen corpses of homeless people who slept on the grates that covered warm-air vents. It was a portent of things to come, such as supplying weapons to Ayatollah Khomeini in Iran and Saddam Hussein in Iraq, waging a secret war in Nicaragua, and vetoing sanctions against South African apartheid. When his secretary of state, General Alexander Haig, publicly suggested that nuns in El Salvador had provoked their rape and murder by forces America supported there, Daniel and I made plans to leave the country. Shortly before we sold our house and departed for Italy in September of 1985, DC Mayor Marion Barry declared a day to be Daniel Ingram Day, to honor Daniel's work to combat poverty and increase opportunities for minority businesses and employees.

Chapter Thirteen

Back to Mississippi

Before leaving for the "Magnolia State," I called Rev. Ann Parker, an NAACP official and church pastor in Moss Point, to tell her that I had been an SNCC worker there in 1964, that I was coming back to see how things were fifty years later, and that I hoped to connect with people who might have been active in the civil rights movement back then. I told her that I had chosen to ask her, specifically, for help because the most dynamic Moss Point woman I had known in '64 was a Mrs. Parker and I thought there might be a connection between the two Mrs. Parkers. Rev. Ann told me that she had been away at school during Freedom Summer and wasn't an eyewitness then, but she had heard about the other Mrs. Parker and would do her best to locate some who were active back then and might have known her, or simply others I might want to get in touch with. We kept in touch by cell phone as Daniel and I slowly made our way down the Atlantic coastline, stopping for a day or two from time to time to enjoy the view of the full moon over the water and the sunset on the other horizon as summer gave way to autumn.

Water always refreshes our spirits, and we enjoyed the ferry rides and the still splendid isolation of the Outer Banks island on which we had pitched a tent and tumbled in the surf fifty years earlier.

This only slightly trammeled beauty enabled us to get past the dreadful approach to Charleston and that once-fair city's occupation by hordes of aging white men in shorts accompanied by wives attired in mass-produced garments that looked like they had been hastily stitched together and affixed with a "designer" label in Asian sweatshops. Daniel thought that the scarcity of African Americans and hotels on South Carolina's shoreline probably resulted from the plethora of private condos and high-rise clubs that were probably exempt from fair-housing laws. But in Savannah, Georgia, we were pleasantly surprised by the number of interracial couples we saw.

We arrived at the strip of highway that separates Moss Point and Pascagoula, Mississippi, in late September of 2013, to find that the towns I had lived and worked in no longer existed, at least not as I remembered them. Both had been almost literally blown off the map in 2005 by Hurricane Katrina. Before that storm, Moss Point was a small town of pines and shade trees with wooden houses on small plots lining quiet streets. It was flanked by rivers and what I thought of as a swamp, but the center of town was earthy in every sense of the word. I had walked and driven down every block in the township when I lived there and I don't remember ever having gotten lost. Adjacent and much larger Pascagoula was a resort community on the Gulf of Mexico that had grown rapidly to become a major shipbuilding port, mainly producing warships for the US Navy. Its sprawling shipyards and expanded neighborhoods made it a difficult place to know well in a short time, but it still had a sleepy coastal ambiance when I worked there in 1964.

In between the restored towns, eight years after Katrina, Daniel and I cringed in our car as we rolled through a suburban looking landscape slashed in every direction by super highways littered with the fast-food stops, gas stations, and chain store outlets that garishly compete for customers across America. I began to feel like we were bumper-to-bumper with computerized automatons constantly speeding to and from the same places. Unable to locate familiar landmarks or find any trace of Pine Street, where I had lived in Moss Point with Mr. William and Mrs. Lottie Scott, we checked into one of the several franchised motels and then called Rev. Parker. She told us she had arranged for us to meet in her church at three the next day with a small group of people who were involved in the freedom struggle in the sixties.

That night, at a restaurant on the Gulf in nearby Biloxi, we sat next to a table at which two white women were loudly slamming "Obamacare" as a socialist takeover of medical care that must be fought until it is repealed. Forced to listen to several minutes of frightful misinformation, I finally interrupted to inform the louder of the two that her assertion that the law established "death panels" was not true, and that the provision which had raised that false fear had been removed before the law was passed. The woman's response was to demand to know what country I was from. I told her I was American but had spent my childhood in Europe, to which she said, "We don't want European socialism here." While driving in the area, Daniel and I had seen signs in front of churches reading, "Pray to End Abortion." We had also passed a huge billboard crediting creationism for the crowning of three blond women as Mississippi beauty queens. I was feeling sheepish about intruding in the death-panel woman's private conversation and was thinking that the atmosphere had changed considerably since 1964. The paranoia seemed familiar, but it was expressed as an insistence on a separate reality rather than a separation of races. We breathed a lot easier, however, when a young interracial couple came in and took a table without anyone but us seeming to notice.

The next morning we located Moss Point's handsome new city hall, not far from where the old one had been, and went inside to ask the chief land and property official how we might find the Scotts' former house on Pine Street, explaining that I had lived there during the summer and fall of '64. I told him that we had looked and looked for it but that nothing seemed to be as I remembered. The official,

Mr. Andrew Beamon, a slightly graying African American man with a quietly thoughtful manner, first said how pleased he was to host someone who had been a part of the freedom movement in Moss Point the year that he was born. He then graciously expressed his regret for the confusing alterations to the local landscape that had been imposed by Miss Katrina. Moss Point had been on the outer edge of the hurricane, he said, where the winds were the highest and the destruction caused was most severe. In contrast, he explained, the damage in New Orleans had been caused by flooding when a levee broke after the eye of the storm had passed over the city. After being savaged by Katrina, Pine Street had been superseded by the construction of Martin Luther King Avenue as a broad thoroughfare.

Leaving City Hall, I was surprised to see Burnham Drugstore, where I had gotten into more trouble than I could safely handle by trying with two African American women to integrate the lunch counter after the polls had closed on Election Day in 1964. Daniel and I walked over to look and were even more surprised to see that it still had a lunch counter. Everything was new and shiny, but the zigzag counter had the ageless pizzazz of the art deco era. The biggest change since the time when two friends and I ordered banana splits was the waitresses. In 1964, our waitress was, and could only have been, white, and she had replied to our order by saying, "We don't serve Niggers!" The young woman now taking orders was black and beautiful. I recounted our long-ago escapade to her and she laughed out loud when I told her that my friend's response to the earlier waitress was, "We didn't ask for Niggers, we asked for banana splits."

When we finally located Rev. Parker's church, we met a dozen women and three men who had been active in the struggle for civil rights during the sixties, and they seemed as delighted to welcome me as I was to see them. Emma Miller explained that five northern students had lived with her during Freedom Summer, but she had never heard from any of them again. All of those present had fought for their rights and all thought I was the only rights worker or student who had come back to see how they were faring years later. One woman, Ernestine Black, said it was a "blessing" that I had come so far to meet with them and that the rights movement had given her the confidence to go to college and not be afraid. "I was the first black to integrate the Mississippi Gulf Coast Community College," she said, "and the first to graduate." Another woman, Franzetta Wells Sanders, told how her children were the first to integrate a previously all-white public school and had endured various forms of hostility from teachers and students, much as I and my sisters had experienced in postwar Germany. Her son had also integrated the local youth baseball team, breaking a barrier á la Jackie Robinson. Those were difficult times and difficult actions, she said, but they helped to bring about positive changes in relations between the races.

Some of the men remembered my project director, Tilmon McKeller, and the Catholic priest who wouldn't allow him to take Communion or make confession. One said that even when local blacks were allowed to attend services at that church, they were made to sit in the back and yield their places if there weren't enough of them for whites. He believed that today, although most churches are still largely black or white, everybody can participate on equal terms if they want to. The men and some women also remembered the violent black policeman cynically hired in response to black community pressure. But that bad memory had been supplanted by the exciting fact that Moss Point has since had two black police chiefs and fully integrated staffs. Someone thought that the first black chief might even have attended my Freedom School in Pascagoula.

Already excited by what they had told me, I was thrilled when I learned that I was sitting beside Aneice Liddell, the first and so far the only black woman to serve as mayor of Moss Point. She looked almost too young to have attended the Freedom School, but remembered doing so. Asked if Moss Point's whites had accepted her as their mayor, she conceded that there was no shortage of prejudiced people in Mississippi, but said she campaigned to become the mayor of all the people and that most whites seemed to accept that she served as promised. Attractive, modest, and matter of fact, she embodied a political revolution with a calm and grace that made the old days when Jim Crow reigned seem an aberration.

The person who felt the strongest about the school and remembered it best was Julia Rodgers Holmes, who had lived in the house nearest the school and remembered the terror of the flaming cross placed in front of it by the Klan. She had been fourteen at that time, the eldest of seven children, and was needed at home to help her mother care for her younger siblings. But she came to the school every chance she got, to learn and to help me with the younger children there. She also occasionally helped me carry the charred cross with "FREEDOM" painted on its crossbar when I took it outside in the morning or took it inside in the evening. She said it upset her that every history of the period that she had seen erroneously placed the cross and school in the Mississippi Delta area, instead of in Pascagoula, and that the movie *Mississippi Burning* had put it in front a church. Obviously proud of our school and her experience in it, Julia made me profoundly, almost deliriously happy by telling me, "You instilled such a love of books in me that I became a librarian, and for thirty years, until I retired, I tried to instill that love in others."

Left speechless, I embraced her and we wet one another's cheeks with joyful tears. In a few words, Julia made me feel that I had actually achieved a cherished dream. I had always been unreservedly glad that I gone to Mississippi and been a minor player in a dangerous movement that had accomplished miracles nonviolently. I had been driven to it by my past and a desire encouraged by my father to oppose racism wherever I found it. And I had been healed, transformed, and strengthened by the experience. But I had never before felt that I had made a significant personal contribution, beyond helping a few people to learn to read. Unconsciously, I had imparted to Julia something of great value to me, and she had in turn imparted it to others.

All of the people in the meeting remembered how difficult and dangerous it had been to gain the rights they now enjoyed and were determined that there would be no going back. They were aware that the presidency of Barack Obama had brought to the surface racism that had gone underground for a time and had burrowed into new locations while there. They were also aware that national forces were supporting gerrymandering and voter suppression measures, such as Mississippi's new voter ID requirement. But, like Israelis, they were used to being under attack and confident that they could overcome their attackers. Besides, they seemed to see most local whites as reasonably friendly and accepting of integration as the established, if not natural, order. One person even ventured that local whites were not as disturbing to him or her as local blacks who had prospered so much that they'd divorced themselves from the problems of the black community.

Our friends appeared to have done so well with their voting rights and seemed so strong and confident that we left Mississippi jubilant in the belief that the new era was here to stay, at least in the southeast corner of Mississippi. On the way home we stopped in Savannah, Georgia, and saw scores of interracial couples, far more than one sees in much larger DC, attracting no more notice than others. It was not until we got back to DC that we remembered that the Voting Rights Act had been eviscerated by the Supreme Court, and that the next day—as dissenting Justice Ruth Bader Ginsburg had predicted—Mississippi enacted previously banned restrictions on voting rights. We feared that our new friends were more exposed to unfriendly fire than they had been in almost fifty years. We called and wrote to them, not to sound an alarm but to try to gauge whether they had been unwilling to express their concerns to their guests. We found that some thought conditions were more problematic than they had acknowledged. But they were not frightened; they were determined. When we had been there, they were still assessing the damage that would be caused by new ID requirements, which would adversely affect older people who didn't have birth certificates, driver's licenses, or deed or rental contracts because of the oppressive conditions in which they had grown up. They hadn't raised the issue with us because they hadn't yet settled on a strategy to counter this outrage. But they confidently assured us they would.

Our new friend Andrew Beamon said that many elderly white people didn't respect black officials and that "skinheads" and other hate groups would probably always be a problem. But he said that in addition to working at City Hall, he was a Sunday school teacher, and he had faith in the future because children were attending integrated Head Start programs and integrated elementary and high schools and learning to judge one another by the content of their character rather than their color. As the old ones pass on and the young ones appear, he said, we will achieve Martin Luther King', Jr. dream in Mississippi.

* * *

Ironically, Mississippi may in fact lead the way toward racial justice. Thanks to the Voting Rights Act of 1965, it leads in the number of black elected officials, and one of the first things I noticed when I arrived in the state's southeast corner in 1964 was that residential areas were much more integrated than DC's suburbs or inner-city. I don't know whether Hurricane Katrina scrambled or separated blacks and whites, but I fervently hope demographics there favor Dr. King's and Mr. Beamon's dream. But as much as I like and share Mr. Beamon's vision of racism diminishing as young people grow up together—integration does indeed beat segregation—and much as I revel in the never-again spirit of the women and men of Moss Point who fought for and will never surrender their rights, my experience with racism, roughly chronicled here, suggests that difficult times, possibly much worse times, could lie ahead. Legally enforced segregation and openly expressed racism may be virtually dead, but racial separation and ghettoization remain virtually unchallenged and invisible to whites except as places to be avoided. Some of the more gifted ghetto wall-climbers have escaped to become the new freedmen and women, and their success should make it easier for others, although it seems unlikely there will soon be another black president, given the white consensus that Barack Obama has unleashed more ills than fabled Pandora. However, those left behind in barrios, ghettos, reservations, and prisons are held back by refashioned obstacles and old-fashioned problems, several of which, such as impartial review of questionable police conduct, are coming to a head at a time of almost incredible international savagery and race-based polarity at home.

Outlawed barriers to voting have been redesigned by computers, rebranded as restrictions on voter fraud, and put into the hands of politicians in every part of the country who seek to advance themselves by holding nonwhites back. Other Jim Crow props, such as farming out convict labor, have been rebirthed by placing convicts in for-profit prisons and enforcing draconian laws in a blatantly color-conscious manner. Everyone knows that nonwhites are a hell of a lot more likely than whites to be shot, killed, incarcerated, or executed. The statistical disparities are stupefying and would, I think, be impossible unless large numbers of whites believed with the founding fathers that blacks are not as inherently entitled as whites are to the blessings of America. Such notions of superiority, whether based on evolution or creationism, are neither new nor original. In one version or another, they have been drummed into callow heads for millennia, reaching a deranged crescendo with the murder of millions during my childhood in Germany.

There are undoubtedly many more American whites today than ever before who don't subscribe to any theory of racial superiority and are generally fair-minded and charitable. They most likely have African American friends or even relatives whom they trust and admire. Many in this group, however, have bought the ideas that blacks reject good jobs to live on the backs of taxpayers, that their poverty results from misconduct or bad choices or both, that they will convert aid to children into money for drugs or alcohol, and that the nation that enslaved and exploited their forbears owes them nothing but the same tilted playing field and corrupt referees they have known for hundreds of years. Since blacks now have their equality, the self-styled opponents of big government maintain, those in need have only themselves to blame for their misfortune and must tough it out like everybody else in this land of fabulous opportunity.

One thing that is new since the passage of civil rights acts in the sixties is the claim by those seeking to extend the benefits of their prior advantages that they are merely defending racial equality against reverse discrimination, an argument that has been warmly embraced by so-called conservatives on the Supreme Court. Forgive me, but this always reminds me of the German corporations that said it would be unfair to make them compensate Jews who had been cruelly used as slave laborers some fifty years earlier during World War II. Today's stockholders shouldn't have to pay for such earlier offenses, they argued, even though the records of slavery had only recently become available. This outrage was aggravated, in my mind, when syndicated columnist Charles Krauthammer, in an article in the *Washington Post,* sided with the corporations and asserted that it would be ungenerous and therefore un-Jewish of Jewish ex- slaves to press their claims so long after their servitude.

With respect to so-called affirmative action, it may be acceptable to argue that even a little bit of racism, like a small malignant tumor, is unacceptable, not just as a matter of abstract principle but as a practical threat. Racism may seem to have been cured or be dormant or appear benign, and then almost inexplicably start to spread, attack vital organs, and metastasize. Almost all of my mother's family and many others perished because they didn't correctly evaluate the danger inherent in modern German racism and flee in time, although some tried and were thwarted by racism elsewhere. But there are many diseases that can be prevented by inoculation, and others may be fought by draining the swamp, chemotherapy, radiation, or drugs that may carry the risk of less harmful side effects. No sensible person can believe that virulent racism was eradicated in the sixties by the civil rights movement and laws passed to curb some of its more harmful effects. And those of us who were naive enough to believe that the election of a black president might usher in a new era of tolerance and progress toward the America that Dr. King and Mr. Beamon envisioned have since recovered our senses. Instead of seeing bluebirds flying, we see that Jim Crow, having changed political allegiances, is not endangered, but has spread his wings and, with more than a little help from friends on the Supreme Court, is soaring over areas far away from Dixie. Our hopes now seem to rest on the shoulders of generations still young or yet to come. We also have to hope there will be time for them to mature and take charge.

The rapid growth in support of gay rights has been inspiring for those who want to reverse the relentless expansion of inequality and find a cure for addiction to weapons that kill. Celebration of a sudden outgrowth of tolerance is important at a time when racism, religious fanaticism, and greed have spawned globalized insanity that is potentially more deadly than the madness that made an abattoir of the twentieth century.

It's often said that those who don't learn from history are doomed to relive it. That, of course, is double-edged. It sounds like a just fate, and possibly would be if the doomed didn't include children and other innocents—those whose interests are always subordinated by war-makers, ethnic cleansers, and other lunatics. It is because of the belief that remembering might confer some benefit, however slight, that I have written this reminder of some of the terrible consequences of racism and of the need to fight it nonviolently in all its guises.